John Lennon

These and other titles are included in The Importance Of biography series:

THE IMPORTANCE OF

John Lennon

by Stuart A. Kallen

Lucent Books, P.O. Box 289011, San Diego, CA 92198-9011

Library of Congress Cataloging-in-Publication Data

Kallen, Stuart A., 1955–
    John Lennon / by Stuart A. Kallen.
      p. cm. — (The importance of)
Includes bibliographical references (p.   ) and index.
    Summary: Profiles the life and work of John Lennon, his life
in Liverpool, learning rock and roll, becoming a star, Beatlemania, his wife Yoko Ono, and the last years.
    ISBN 1-56006-747-0 (alk. paper)
    1. Lennon, John, 1940–1980—Juvenile literature. 2. Rock
musicians—Biography—Juvenile literature. [1. Lennon, John,
1940–1980. 2. Musicians. 3. Rock music.] I. Title. II. Series.
    ML3930.L34 K35 2002
    782.42166'092—dc21

                                                    2001000982

Contents

Foreword

THE IMPORTANCE OF biography series deals with individuals who have made a unique contribution to history. The editors of the series have deliberately chosen to cast a wide net and include people from all fields of endeavor. Individuals from politics, music, art, literature, philosophy, science, sports, and religion are all represented. In addition, the editors did not restrict the series to individuals whose accomplishments have helped change the course of history. Of necessity, this criterion would have eliminated many whose contribution was great, though limited. Charles Darwin, for example, was responsible for radically altering the scientific view of the natural history of the world. His achievements continue to impact the study of science today. Others, such as Chief Joseph of the Nez Percé, played a pivotal role in the history of their own people. While Joseph's influence does not extend much beyond the Nez Percé, his nonviolent resistance to white expansion and his continuing role in protecting his tribe and his homeland remain an inspiration to all.

These biographies are more than factual chronicles. Each volume attempts to emphasize an individual's contributions both in his or her own time and for posterity. For example, the voyages of Christopher Columbus opened the way to European colonization of the New World. Unquestionably, his encounter with the New World brought monumental changes to both Europe and the Americas in his day. Today, however, the broader impact of Columbus's voyages is being critically scrutinized. *Christopher Columbus,* as well as every biography in The Importance Of series, includes and evaluates the most recent scholarship available on each subject.

Each author includes a wide variety of primary and secondary source quotations to document and substantiate his or her work. All quotes are footnoted to show readers exactly how and where biographers derive their information, as well as provide stepping stones to further research. These quotations enliven the text by giving readers eyewitness views of the life and times of each individual covered in The Importance Of series.

Finally, each volume is enhanced by photographs, bibliographies, chronologies, and comprehensive indexes. For both the casual reader and the student engaged in research, The Importance Of biographies will be a fascinating adventure into the lives of people who have helped shape humanity's past and present, and who will continue to shape its future.

A Message in Music

John Lennon was a singer, musician, poet, artist, father, and husband. As the leader of the Beatles in the 1960s, his innovative and creative music inspired nearly every other professional musician of that era and encouraged millions of amateurs to pick up guitars, write poetry, and express themselves in song. Even in the twenty-first century—thirty years after the Beatles' breakup—pop stars from the Backstreet Boys to Beck acknowledge Lennon's influence in their music. And with more than 158.5 million albums sold, the Beatles remain the best-selling recording act of all time.

It would be hard to imagine the 1960s without Lennon's contribution to popular culture and the counterculture. Despite tragedies in his personal life, Lennon, whether collaborating with fellow Beatle Paul McCartney or writing solo, wrote music that was witty, enlightening, and positive in a decade marred by wars, riots, and assassinations. And in the process of becoming the world's biggest rock star, he won the hearts of millions.

John Lennon inspired world peace and love with his actions and with songs such as "All You Need Is Love," "Imagine," and "Give Peace a Chance." Songs such as "Strawberry Fields Forever," about lost childhood dreams, became the psychedelic soundtrack to the hippie revolution. In the early 1970s, he was on the forefront of the women's movement with the controversial "Woman Is the Nigger of the World." And, later in that decade, before the term *family values* was a political cliché, Lennon stepped

John Lennon, shown here in 1964, inspired millions in his roles of musician, poet, artist, and family man.

off the merry-go-round of fame and fortune, tuned out the world, and stayed at home to raise his young son Sean.

SONGS OF LOVE

John Lennon sang about war, peace, women's liberation, and revolution. But he most often sang of love—love between man and woman, love between father and child, and, perhaps most important, love for all humanity.

Lennon did more than just sing, however. He contributed millions of dollars and countless hours of his time to the causes he believed in. He risked his fame, fortune, and reputation in attempts to bring peace to the world and equality between people. His efforts were not always successful, and the press found it easy to mock him when he held a "bed-in for peace" or marched with radical antiwar leaders. Unlike some other popular artists of his time, however, Lennon practiced what he preached.

When John Lennon was cut down by an assassin's bullet in 1980, the world was stunned into silence. Few who lived through that event will forget where they were when they heard the news. It was impossible to imagine how someone could kill a genius whose message was so overwhelmingly positive and who was loved so deeply by so many.

Even though the world could not understand the thoughts in the twisted mind of Lennon's assassin, the singer's death again united millions of people—this time in mourning. Spontaneous memorials occurred in cities across the globe as fans gath-

Lennon risked his fame and fortune in attempts to spread love for humanity and peace throughout the world.

ered to light candles, cry, and sing Lennon's songs, once again, in a united voice.

HIS MUSIC LIVES ON

Although John Lennon died in 1980, his music and memory continue to dominate popular culture. In August 2000, the Beatles were honored by the Recording Industry Association of America as the best-selling act of all time. In October of that year, *The Beatles Anthology*, the history of the band by the band, was released with great fanfare. In spite of the book's $60 price tag, it quickly shot to the top of the *New York Times* best-seller list.

The importance of John Lennon was also demonstrated by the continuing hunger for his music. In November 2000, the Beatles released the album *1*, containing twenty-seven songs that were number-one hits in the '60s. The album sold nearly 600,000 copies in the first week after its release and more than 5 million within the following eight weeks.

Although the Beatles broke up in 1970, the sales of *1* topped those of recent pop stars such as Ricky Martin, Britney Spears, the Backstreet Boys, and others. Once again, songs penned by Lennon such as "All You Need Is Love," "The Ballad of John and Yoko," and "Come Together" were topping the charts.

On December 8, 2000, on the twentieth anniversary of Lennon's death, thousands of fans gathered in parks across the globe to honor and celebrate the musician's memory. At Strawberry Fields, an area in New York City's Central Park dedicated to Lennon, hundreds of fans gathered to

Fans from all over the world celebrated Lennon's memory on the twentieth anniversary of his death. These fans in New York City gathered at Strawberry Fields, an area of Central Park dedicated to Lennon.

sing his songs. In Lennon's hometown of Liverpool, an English Heritage plaque was mounted on his childhood home.

In Havana, Cuba, President Fidel Castro presented a bronze statue of the former Beatle in the newly created John Lennon Park. While Castro called Lennon a revolutionary, one of the speakers put it more eloquently. Ricardo Alarcón, head of the Cuban congress, said, "Dear John, there were many people who said, on Dec. 8, 20 years ago [when you were shot] that an era [of peace and love] had ended. But your message will never end."[1]

With the Beatles' continuing popularity, John Lennon's music remains nearly as popular today as it was when it was new. And although Lennon's life was cut short in 1980, his positive and influential message lives forever in music.

1 Life in Liverpool

John Winston Lennon, a man whose music would generate nearly a decade of rock 'n' roll hysteria, was born in Liverpool, England, at a time of chaos. On October 9, 1940, as John's mother, Julia, was giving birth, war planes from Nazi Germany were conducting violent bombing raids on Lennon's home town.

As explosions shook the city and flames lit up the night sky, Julia's sister Mary "Mimi" Stanley rushed to the Oxford Street maternity home to see her new nephew John. Mimi held the baby in her arms as a bomb fell directly outside the hospital. For protection, little Johnny was placed under the bed until quiet fell upon the city. In this moment of joy and tragedy, Julia gave her newborn son the middle name Winston to honor Winston Churchill, the prime minister of Great Britain.

FIVE BEAUTIFUL WOMEN

The birth of John Lennon was a momentous occasion for his family. But like the havoc that rained down on Liverpool at that moment, it was a sad one as well. John's father, Fred Lennon, was nowhere to be found.

John's mother, pretty, smart, and witty, had met Fred in 1938 before the beginning of World War II. Fred was occasionally employed as a lowly ship's waiter, and Julia's family was greatly concerned when she married him on impulse after a short courtship. To her four sisters it seemed as if Julia had married Fred only to annoy their strict father. After the marriage ceremony, according to Mimi, "Julia came home, threw [the marriage license] on the table and said, 'There, that's it. I've married him.'"[2]

Soon after they married, Fred found work on a passenger liner that sailed to America. When the war broke out between England and Germany in 1939, Fred was on a ship docked in New York City. He returned to Liverpool for a short time in 1940 and then disappeared again. This would become a pattern during John's early life.

With her husband gone most of the time, Julia took John to live with the Stanley family. All four of her sisters helped raise John but it was Mimi who took special care of the baby boy. John, who would later become a great champion of women's liberation, recalled those early years:

There were five women that were my family. Five strong, intelligent, beautiful women; five sisters. One happened to be my mother. My mother just couldn't deal with life. She was the youngest and she couldn't cope with me and I ended up living with her elder sister. . . . Those women were fantastic . . . because they dominated the situation in the family.

The men were invisible. I was always with the women. I always heard them talk about men and talk about life, and they always knew what was going on. The men never ever knew. That was my first feminist education.[3]

People of Liverpool sift through the debris after a Nazi air raid. John Lennon was born as bombs fell outside the hospital where he was delivered.

TRAUMATIC EVENTS

While John's aunts may have given him joy, his parents' stormy marriage was a cause of great trauma. Fred would be gone for months at a time, only to return from sea to find that Julia had been dating other men she had met at local pubs. This led to violent confrontations that often ended in fistfights. John, too, was extremely upset by these strange men in his mother's life, and as a little boy he often lashed out in anger, displaying extreme hostility toward his playmates.

When John was four, Fred decided to move to New Zealand and take his son with him. In an emotional confrontation between Fred and Julia, John was asked to decide whether he wanted to go with his mother or father. John said he wanted to be with Fred, but after his mother walked out the door, John ran down the street after her. The matter was settled, and as Fred later recalled, "That was the last I saw or heard from him till I was told he'd become a Beatle."[4]

Although John had chosen his mother, he was taken instead to live with his aunt Mimi and her new husband George Smith on Liverpool's Menlove Avenue. By this time, the war was over, and John's parents were officially divorced. While his parents went their separate ways, John would carry the emotional scars of their bitter marriage for decades. As Albert Goldman writes in *The Lives of John Lennon*,

> By the time little John had settled into his aunt Mimi's home, he . . . had been neglected, uprooted, passed from hand to hand, and finally compelled

to make an impossible choice: either to give up his mother in order to retain his father or to relinquish his father in order to hold on to his mother, who, as it turned out, really didn't want him.[5]

LIFE ON MENLOVE AVENUE

Mimi, a nurse by profession, was fiercely committed to helping Lennon get over his disturbing past. Mimi also ran a strict household and kept a tight control on her nephew's behavior. She personally chose his playmates to make sure they were of good character, and she banned comic books and movie shows—amusements she considered to be of the lower classes.

As for his parents, Lennon was simply told that they were no longer in love. He later said, "I soon forgot my father. It was like he was dead. But I did see my mother now and again and my feeling never died off for her. I often thought about her, though I never realized for a long time that she was living no more than five or ten miles away."[6]

Even though Lennon may have longed for his mother, his life was comfortable. His uncle George helped him learn to read and write at the age of four. To do so, Smith perched John on his knee and read through the Liverpool newspaper with him. As Mimi said, "Syllable by syllable, George would work at him till he got it right. . . . My husband went through all the headlines in the newspaper with John every night."[7] Lennon would later use newspaper headlines as inspiration for his lyrics, most notably the song "A Day in the Life."

George also taught the little boy to draw and paint, inspiring Lennon to become an artist in later years. And although Mimi and George were not musicians, they listened to music all day long on a radio-phonograph. George even hooked up an extension speaker with a long wire so that Lennon could hear the classical music and radio shows while lying on the bed in his tiny upstairs room.

At age four, John's uncle taught him to read with Liverpool newspapers. Later, John and the Beatles would appear on the front pages of newspapers.

Like all little boys, Lennon also loved to play in the backyard. But even before he started kindergarten, he seemed to be a born leader. When he played cowboys and Indians with his friends, Mimi recalled, "He had to be in charge. Always. The other boys had to be cowboys and he *had* to be the Indian. And when he said they were dead, they were dead. 'Pretend properly,' he would tell them."[8]

WRITING HIS OWN BOOKS

When John Lennon was five years old, he began taking classes at Dovedale Primary School near Liverpool's Penny Lane. He was highly skilled at reading, writing, and even making puns. He playfully turned words around, writing "funs" for "funds" and "chicken pots" for "chicken pox."

Although he had chronically bad eyesight, Lennon used his artistic and writing skills to compose his own stories. According to Philip Norman in *Shout*, "At the age of seven, he began writing books of his own. One of them was called *Sport and Speed Illustrated*; it had cartoons and drawings and a serial story ending: 'If you liked this, come again next week. It'll be even better.'"[9]

Away from school Lennon was also expanding his horizons, making friends with some local neighborhood boys. Pete Shotton, who lived around the corner from Lennon, was his first best friend. Several other boys joined up with Lennon and Shotton and formed a young gang whose members quickly became known as neighborhood troublemakers. Ever the leader, Lennon would instruct the boys to break streetlights, steal toys from local shops, and create other mischief.

With his exceptional intelligence and leadership abilities, Lennon stood out among his classmates. Boyhood friend Doug Freeman recalled,

> To me, he . . . always stuck out as somebody different, even from the age of five or six. Whatever he did, he was going to be unusual. If there was anything out of the ordinary going on in the school it was centred on him. You definitely noticed him, even at that age. He was on a totally different wavelength from the others, and although he was sometimes causing trouble and disagreements, as kids do, no teachers could ever [figure out] what it was about him that was different. It stuck out a mile. The teachers could never tie him down to anything. He was always the centre of attention; he was different from anyone else in the school.[10]

QUARRY BANK GRAMMAR SCHOOL

At the age of twelve Lennon entered the Quarry Bank Grammar School, located about a mile from his home. Every morning he would pedal his Raleigh bicycle up the long hill to the school, dressed in the new black blazer Mimi had commissioned her husband's tailor to make for the boy. Over the breast pocket of the blazer a red and gold badge displayed an embroidered stag's head and the school's motto written in Latin: "From this rough metal we forge virtue."[11] By this time John Lennon was indeed "rough metal," or as some might call him, a full-fledged juvenile delinquent. According to Pete Shotton, "We went through [Quarry Bank] together like Siamese twins. . . . We started in our first year at the top and gradually sank together into the subbasement."[12]

Like many English schools of the time, Quarry Bank was populated by teachers, called masters, who wore mortarboard caps and long black gowns. Student monitors, known as prefects, kept strict watch over students and administered harsh punishment by swatting the buttocks of offenders with long whiplike canes. Lennon often found himself the target of these canings and was sometimes reduced to crawling away on his hands and knees after such punishment.

Lennon's bad attitude toward life escalated considerably at the age of thirteen when his beloved uncle George died suddenly from a brain hemorrhage. As Paul McCartney later said, "John began to think that there was a jinx on the male side [of the family]: father left home, uncle dead."[13]

To hide the pain of his loss, Lennon, and his ever-present sidekick Shotton became the bad boys of their school, smoking cigarettes, disrupting class, stealing, swearing, and fighting. Lennon later commented on his fighting techniques:

> I looked at all the hundreds of . . . kids [at Quarry Bank Grammar School] and thought, "Christ, I'll have to fight all my way through this lot." There was some real heavies there. The first fight I got in, I lost. I lost my nerve when I got really hurt. Not that there was much real fighting; I did a lot of swearing and shouting, then got a

quick punch. If there was a bit of blood, then you packed it in.

> I was aggressive because I wanted to be popular. I wanted to be the leader. . . . I wanted everybody to do what I told them to do, to laugh at my jokes and let me be the boss.[14]

John Lennon's offenses at Quarry Bank were many. According to Norman, they included "insolence"; "throwing blackboard [erasers] out of windows"; "cutting class and going AWOL (absent without leave)"; and "gambling on [the] school field during [a sports] match."[15]

Lennon's report cards reflected similar concerns. According to Shotton, "'Wasted intelligence,' 'clown in class,' 'shocking,' and 'hopeless' were but a few of the epithets our masters were apt to bandy about in summing up our academic performance."[16]

Part of Lennon's problem was that he was a brilliant and creative teenager attending a school whose curriculum hadn't changed since the nineteenth century. In this stifling atmosphere, there was little outlet for a young man who would later prove himself to be one of the most talented songwriters and musicians in the world. Lennon later stated, "I used to think . . . 'I'm a genius or I'm mad. Which is it? I can't be mad because nobody's put me away— therefore I'm a genius.' I mean genius is a form of madness. . . . Genius is pain, too. It's just pain."[17]

A DEVELOPING ARTIST

Even though Lennon's grades remained well below average and he was the bane

THE CLASS CLOWN

John Lennon and his best friend Pete Shotton were known throughout Quarry Bank Grammar School for their outrageous pranks, as Shotton describes in John Lennon in My Life.

"It didn't take us very long to establish our credentials as our class's resident clowns. We thought nothing of hiding alarm clocks, timed to go off in the middle of a lesson, at the bottom of our school satchels, or filling a bicycle pump with ink to squirt at our less vigilant masters when their backs were turned, or rigging up the blackboard to collapse the instant the teacher began writing on it.

Whenever John and I could arrange it, others ended up shouldering the blame for our misdeeds. After making the discovery that the pillars in one of our classrooms were hollow and could be pried open, we decided to inter [put inside] a particularly meek and obliging classmate just before French class. (According to tradition, the teacher always made his grand entrance at the sound of the bell, by which time the boys were all supposed to be at [their] desks.) Halfway through the lesson, our victim apparently fainted from lack of air, and fell out of the wall with a resounding crash.

'Simmons!' barked the French master. 'Get to your place and stop fooling about!' Though the dazed Simmons would never have dared point the finger at us, eventually we too got in trouble because we couldn't stop ourselves from chuckling over the success of our prank.

With our talent for accumulating black marks, John and I grew accustomed to being kept after school several days a week."

of his schoolmasters, he continued to express himself through art, poetry, stories, and music. The last forty minutes of the school day was known as "prep" period, a time when a student could study or scribble in a notebook. Lennon spent his prep time filling scraps of paper with cartoons, stories, and poems. He used his favorite book, *Alice in Wonderland* by Lewis Carroll, as a model for his words and pictures, later saying, "I was passionate about *Alice in Wonderland* and drew all the characters. I did poems in the style of 'Jabberwocky' [a Carroll Poem that uses nonsensical language]. I used to love Alice."[18]

Drawing on Carroll's verse for inspiration, Lennon wrote short stories with titles such as "The Land of the Lunapots" and "Tales of Hermit Fred." In typical Lennon style, they were full of word play, puns, jokes, and twisted humor. Ray Coleman provides an example of word play in this untitled poem written when the young man was fifteen:

> Owl George ee be a farmer's lad
> With mucklekak and cow
> Ee be the son of 'is owl Dad
> But why I don't know how
>
> Ee tak a fork and bale the hay
> And stacking-stook he stock
> And lived his loif from day to day
> Dressed in a sweaty sock. . . .
>
> Our Nellie be a gal so fine
> All dimpled wart and blue
> She herds the pigs, the rotten swine
> It mak me wanna spew![19]

Mimi was less than impressed with Lennon's poetry and writing. She wanted him to become a respectable professional such as a veterinarian or pharmacist. She even attempted to throw away her nephew's stories and artwork, some of which was obscene. When the fourteen-year-old Lennon caught her, he told her, "Don't you destroy my papers. . . . One day I'll be famous and you're going to regret it."[20]

As far as music was concerned, Lennon had been playing the harmonica, or "mouth organ," since he was about nine years old. He could quickly learn new songs, and those who heard him play were often impressed. On one occasion, Lennon was playing the harmonica on a bus and the bus driver liked it so much he gave him a very expensive harmonica, which further fueled the budding musician's creativity.

Through it all, Julia moved in and out of her son's life. As Lennon got older, he would often spend the weekend at his mother's house after fighting with Mimi. During this time, Julia taught her wayward son to play the banjo. Norman describes Lennon's renewed relationship with Julia:

> John, as he grew older, grew more and more fascinated by this pretty auburn-haired woman, so much more like an elder sister than a mother. For Julia did not echo the dire warnings given by Aunt Mimi and Quarry Bank. Julia encouraged him to live for the present, as she did, and for laughter and practical jokes. . . .
>
> Julia thought as John and Pete did, and told them the things they wanted to hear. She told them not to worry about school or homework or what their lives might have in store.[21]

ROCK AND ROLL COMES TO ENGLAND

Encouraged by his mother, Lennon practically made a career of being a rebellious teenager. But he certainly was not the only defiant youth in Liverpool in the mid-1950s. After World War II, millions of children were born to returning soldiers and their wives. By the late 1950s, these children, called "baby boomers," were reaching their

"JABBERWOCKY"

John Lennon often spoke of the great influence the classic children's story Alice in Wonderland *by Lewis Carroll had on his poetry, music, and art. The song "I Am the Walrus," for instance, was inspired by the Carroll poem "The Walrus and the Carpenter." But Lennon's favorite poem, from* The Complete Works of Lewis Carroll, *was the nonsensical "Jabberwocky," in which Carroll describes a boy slaying a mythical animal known as the "Jabberwock." Carroll's poem was punctuated with invented words such as* frumious *and* slithy *that sounded pleasing to the ear.*

Lewis Carroll's creative and nonsensical writing greatly influenced Lennon's poetry, music, and art.

"'Twas brillig, and the slithy toves
Did gyre and gimble in the wabe;
All mimsy were the borogoves,
And the mome raths outgrabe.

'Beware the Jabberwock, my son!
The jaws that bite, the claws that catch!
Beware the Jubjub bird, and shun
The frumious Bandersnatch!'

He took his vorpal sword in hand:
Long time the manxome foe he sought—
So rested he by the Tumtum tree,
And stood awhile in thought.
And, as in uffish thought he stood,
The Jabberwock, with eyes of flame,
Came whiffling through the tulgey wood,
And burbled as it came!

One two! One two! And through and through
The vorpal blade went snicker-snack!
He left it dead, and with its head
He went galumphing back.

'And hast thou slain the Jabberwock?
Come to my arms, my beamish boy!
O frabjous day! Callooh! Callay!'
He chortled in his joy.

'Twas brillig, and the slithy toves
Did gyre and gimble in the wabe;
All mimsy were the borogoves,
And the mome raths outgrabe."

teenage years and rebellion was in the air. Adding fuel to that fire was American rock and roll by artists such as Chuck Berry, Little Richard, and Elvis Presley.

It began in 1955 when an American movie called *The Blackboard Jungle* was released in Britain. When the song "Rock Around the Clock" by Bill Haley and the Comets was played during the film, riots broke out in the movie theaters. When Haley later toured England, fans mobbed the pudgy musician, exhibiting unprecedented hysteria in a country known for its conservative and reserved populace.

In February 1956, Elvis Presley's first single, "Heartbreak Hotel," was released in Britain. It immediately shot to the top of the record charts and remained there for nearly five months. This song was followed by "Blue Suede Shoes" and then by "Hound Dog." Presley's songs affected English teenagers as much as they did their American counterparts, causing girls to swoon with love and boys to imitate the mannerisms and style of their rock hero. Most English adults, on the other hand, were appalled at the hold the music had over their children.

Musicians Bill Haley (left) and Elvis Presley brought rock and roll to the formerly conservative youth of Britain. Young Lennon became smitten with Elvis after hearing "Heartbreak Hotel."

Norman explains how this music, inspired by rhythm and blues, was perceived by adults:

> To Britain, as to America, the idea that a white man could sing like a black man was intrinsically lewd. It confirmed the malignant power of rock and roll music to incite young people, as jungle drums incited savages, to . . . violence, promiscuity, disobedience and disrespect. To Britain, as to America, there was only one consolation. A thing so grotesque as Elvis Presley could not possibly last. They [the adults] said [that in] six months, it would all be over.[22]

Teenagers, however, knew instinctively that rock and roll was not just a passing fad—especially when the music inspired new styles of dress and behavior. Young men who previously attended school in short pants, ties, and black blazers began to wear their hair brushed up from their forehead, greased back in Elvis's pompadour style. Those who could afford it also dressed in long black or blue velvet coats, known as drape jackets, modeled on the rakish style of England's turn-of-the-century King Edward III. Since Edward was nicknamed Ted, the fashion plates dubbed themselves Teddy Boys. Even the name was considered controversial at the time. As Shotton writes, "In class-conscious Britain, one of the most truly subversive aspects of the Teddy Boys was the manner in which these working-class ruffians parodied the dress of a previous generation's aristocracy."[23]

"NOTHING ELSE BUT ROCK 'N' ROLL"

The popularity of rock and roll and Teddy Boy fashion suddenly made John Lennon a rebel with a cause. From the moment he heard "Heartbreak Hotel," the young man was smitten. He began playing Elvis records nonstop, and talked about him constantly. As Mimi later said, "From then on . . . I never got a minute's peace. It was Elvis Presley, Elvis Presley, Elvis Presley."[24] Lennon put it more succinctly: "Once I heard [Elvis] and got into it, that was life, there was no other thing. I thought of nothing else but rock 'n' roll."[25]

Lennon also adopted Teddy Boy fashions, cutting school with Shotton to hang around the Liverpool docks, staring in wonder at the tough sailors on leave dressed in full Teddy Boy regalia. Although Mimi would not let Lennon dress as a real Teddy Boy—sending him to school in his standard black blazer—Julia bought him brightly colored shirts and paid for a tailor to narrow his pant legs into the popular skin-tight "drainpipe" style.

Meanwhile, another type of music, known as skiffle, grabbed Lennon's attention. Skiffle was based on 1920s American "jug band" music played by poverty-stricken musicians, often to raise money for rent. Skiffle was performed on homemade instruments such as crude guitars and banjos made from wooden cigar boxes and gourds. The musicians also blew into comb-and-paper kazoos, thumped the beat on a washtub bass, blew low notes into whiskey jugs, ran violin bows across musical saws, and clacked out the rhythm with

TEDDY BOYS

John Lennon was part of the Teddy Boy movement of the late 1950s. A website maintained by the Crazy Cavan 'n' the Rhythm Rockers (www.rockabilly.nl/gener-al/teddyboys.htm) gives the history of the "Teds."

"The Teddyboy emerged in the 1950s [when working-] class teenagers could for the first time afford good clothes, a bicycle or motorcycle and entertainment. The clothing that the Teddyboys wore was designed to shock their parents' generation. It consisted of an Edwardian style drape jacket [a long jacket with velvet collar and cuffs] . . . suede Gibson shoes with thick crepe soles, narrow 'drainpipe' trousers, a smart shirt and a [very narrow, brightly colored] tie. . . . The trademark drape jacket was not as impractical as it seems. Not only did it act as a badge of recognition but, as it was made of woollen cloth with lots of pockets, it kept its owner warm as he hung around in the street and was also good at concealing weapons and alcohol. The Teddygirls adopted American fashions such as toreador [bullfighter] pants and circle skirts, although they tended to wear low cut tops to make themselves look less prissy. Girls wore ponytails and the boys tried a number of experimental hairstyles, the most favourite being the overblown [pompadour] with a [tail known as a] DA (ducks arse) at the back.

The Teds fully embraced the American Rock and Roll music that hit Britain and the British bands that adopted the same style. The Teds were, however, shadowy figures at the dancehalls, lurking around the bars, bopping around and drinking. They formed gangs who sometimes had a common uniform like a particular colour of jacket or socks. For the most part, violence and vandalism was not too serious by modern standards, and exaggerated by the media, but there were instances of serious gang warfare with razors and knives."

spoons, bones, or thimble-capped fingers on washboards.

In 1956 a musician named Lonnie Donegan started the English skiffle craze when he reworked the 1930s American folk song "Rock Island Line." When the song shot to number one, washboard factories had to work overtime to keep up with the demand. And even the poorest teenager could attach a broomstick to a wash bucket, tighten some clothesline across the pole, and come up with a crude wash-tub bass.

A young man of John Lennon's reputation, however, was not about to settle for an old tub. He began an incessant plea for money from both Mimi and Julia so that he could buy a guitar. There is some dispute as to which one of the sisters finally gave in, but soon enough Lennon was the proud owner of a cheap guitar and plenty of rock-and-roll spirit.

LEARNING TO PLAY

For the next several months Lennon emerged from his bedroom only to eat or go to school.

Skiffle bands, based on American "jug bands" from the 1920s, caught Lennon's attention in 1956 and inspired him to buy his first guitar.

The rest of his waking hours were spent hunched over his guitar learning to play songs such as Buddy Holly's "That'll Be the Day" and Chuck Berry's "Johnny B. Goode," among others. Meanwhile, Mimi would chide him: "The guitar's all right for a hobby, John, but you'll never make a living at it."[26] But Lennon had other plans, and after many months of living, breathing, and even dreaming rock and roll, the Liverpool Teddy Boy was about to make his mark on England and the world.

Chapter

2 Learning to Rock and Roll

By 1957 the rock-and-roll music of Elvis Presley, Buddy Holly, Carl Perkins, Gene Vincent, and Chuck Berry had changed the lives of millions of British teenagers. The normally conservative British press dubbed this new movement a "youthquake" as thousands of teenage boys—and a few girls—picked up guitars and learned to play.

John Lennon was among those teens, and in his seventeenth year he put aside nearly everything else in his life to learn music. As his boyhood friend Nigel Whalley said, "He'd sit on his bed, just strumming. . . . Strumming the . . . chords [his mother] Julia had shown him, and singing words that came into his head. After about ten minutes, he'd have got a tune going."[27]

Despite his budding talent, Lennon did not immediately dream of becoming a rock star like his hero Elvis Presley. Although the young man tried to emulate Elvis's dress, style, and sneer, he did not even consider the possibility that he could become an international star. As Lennon's best friend Pete Shotton wrote,

> It would have seemed inconceivable to us that a boy of limited means from the provinces of England might emulate the professional achievements of a Bill

Haley or an Elvis. To make real music, after all, one first had to have the money to buy expensive equipment and instruments—and these, moreover, presumably required years of tedious lessons and practice to master. Above all, rock & roll stars were—almost by definition—American.[28]

THE QUARRY MEN

Rock stars may have been Americans, but the skiffle craze led by Englishman Lonnie Donegan was definitely a homegrown affair. When Donegan appeared on English TV playing American folk songs at breakneck speed, Lennon—and thousands of others—found a musical hero he could emulate. As Shotton said, "Lonnie Donegan's unspoken message . . . was you didn't have to be a 'professional' to play pop music."[29]

As a boy who had always made himself the center of attention, it was only natural that Lennon would form his own skiffle group. Rather than find skilled musicians, who might dispute his role as the leader, Lennon simply recruited the nonmusical Shotton to back him up.

Lennon found a musician he could emulate in Englishman Lonnie Donegan. After seeing Donegan perform on television, Lennon formed his own skiffle group.

Shotton found an old washboard in his parents' garden shed and bought some thimbles for his fingers so that he could loudly strum out a rhythm on the board's ridged glass face. The duo rehearsed in Lennon's mother's bathroom—standing in the bathtub—where the echoing sound reminded them of the reverb heard on early rock records. Their repertoire consisted of American folk songs Donegan had made popular such as "Rock Island Line," "Wabash Cannonball," and "Cumberland Gap." And whereas Americans constructed basses from metal washtubs, in typically British fashion,

Lennon and Shotton constructed a stand-up bass from a tea chest—a wooden box used for holding tea.

The boys persuaded some other childhood friends to join them in the new group, which they named the Quarry Men in honor of their school and the many sandstone quarries that surrounded their neighborhood. Len Garry was persuaded to thump on the tea-chest bass, and Rod Davis was asked to join mainly because he owned a banjo and could play a few chords. When Garry didn't have time to play bass, Ivan Vaugh was brought in. Eric

Griffiths was encouraged to join because he owned a brand-new guitar—and he knew a real drummer, Colin Hanton, who had just bought an expensive new drum set. Norman describes Lennon's role: "In the group, as in the gang, John was the undisputed leader. His plaid shirt collar turned up, Teddy Boy style, scowling like Elvis, he monopolized the foreground and the microphone, if there chanced to be one."[30]

Although the Quarry Men attempted to play Elvis songs, they did not learn the proper words because they could not afford to buy the expensive records. And since the records were rarely played on the BBC, the government-owned radio station,

---

MYTHICAL AMERICAN MUSIC

In the late 1950s, John Lennon and his best friend Pete Shotton considered the United States to be a fantasyland of the rich and famous. This belief was fueled by their interest in rock and roll. However, the budding musicians could rarely hear American rock records because the government controlled the only radio stations. Shotton explains in John Lennon in My Life:

"We all regarded the States, in those days, not only as the leader of the Western world, but also as a remote, mythical place—almost a fantasyland. Since nobody we knew had ever traveled there, our impressions of the country were drawn largely from Hollywood—especially Westerns and gangster films—and from such [typical] American exports as blue jeans and Coca-Cola. All the evidence convinced us that the U.S.A. was a futuristic paradise of fast cars, fast food, fast money, and fast women—a society infinitely more permissive and exciting than our own. From our vantage point, at least, rock & roll music represented the [embodiment] of this American dream.

Hearing the music, however, was no simple matter. We counted ourselves lucky when a BBC program . . . aired a single original Presley number. . . . Neither were many American rock records readily available in the shops or anywhere. . . . As far as John and I were concerned, Liverpool in the mid-fifties was as out of touch as a city could possibly be. . . .

Our salvation proved to be Radio Luxembourg, which boasted a late-night program, 'The Jack Jackson Show,' devoted primarily to original American rock & roll recordings. Whenever Mr. Jackson was scheduled to hold forth, John and I would sit up in our respective beds with our radios pressed to our ears, straining through the intervening static for authentic snatches of Elvis Presley, Bill Haley, and Gene Vincent."

Lennon simply made up his own words to the songs. He used similar methods in his guitar playing. When he broke a guitar string, as he often did because of his rough playing style, he simply grabbed Davis's banjo out of his arms. While Lennon finished the song, Davis would kneel down on the floor to change his bandmate's broken guitar string.

FIRST GIGS

Although none of Lennon's teenage gang could play very well, their old friend Nigel Whalley had even less musical talent than the rest. As such, Whalley was given the role of manager of the Quarry Men, and he even had business cards printed up that read,

Country. Western. Rock 'n' Roll. Skiffle
The Quarry Men
OPEN FOR ENGAGEMENTS
Nigel Whalley, Manager [31]

For the Quarry Men, the best way to get gigs was to play at amateur skiffle contests. These were held during the ten-minute breaks taken by the professional bands that were playing in big ballrooms all over Liverpool. Transportation for the Quarry Men, however, was a problem, and to get to the contests they often had to travel across Liverpool on buses holding their tea chest, drums, and guitars on their laps as the vehicle crawled through traffic.

Despite their dedication, the Quarry Men never won any contests, so Shotton's mother finally took pity on the boys and got them a gig at the annual garden party at St.

Peter's Church in nearby Woolton. On July 6, 1957, only days before Lennon and Shotton were to graduate high school, the Quarry Men assembled on a small stage in a field behind the church. Realizing that this was an important engagement, Lennon was dressed in full Teddy Boy regalia, with a heavily padded jacket, drainpipe trousers (or "dranies"), a blue and white checked shirt, long sideburns, and an extremely greasy, pompadour hairdo.

Mimi had begun the day lecturing Lennon about his failing grades and his wicked taste in clothing. She had no idea that her young nephew would soon be onstage at St. Peter's, but she attended the fete. She described her feelings when she saw Lennon playing for the first time:

> Well, when I got there and stood talking to young people over a cup of tea, there was suddenly this loud beat—bang, bang, coming from the bottom field. It shook everybody up. . . . All the young people . . . proceeded down to the field. I said: "Where are they going" and my sister said: "There must be a band, let's go."

> [When Mimi saw John, she was transfixed.] I couldn't take my eyes off him. . . . There was this grin all over John's face and then he spotted me walking towards him and his expression changed a bit. I don't know why—I was pleased as punch to see him up there. [32]

Although Lennon was startled when he saw his aunt, his feelings changed when she led the crowd in loud applause at the end of the first number.

PAUL MCCARTNEY'S CHILDHOOD

When Paul McCartney joined forces with John Lennon, the two young musicians laid the groundwork for the Beatles. The website run by Great Britain's National Trust (www.spekehall.org. uk/early_years.htm) describes McCartney's childhood before he met Lennon.

"The McCartneys [were a] happy family . . . [until] the autumn of 1956 [when Paul's mother] Mary began suffering from chest pains and shortly afterwards . . . died of breast cancer. . . . [Paul's father] Jim McCartney was left at the age of 53 to bring up two young boys on £8 a week. Aunts rallied round, and somehow they coped.

[The McCartney home] was always a musical house. Jim had taught himself to play the piano at fourteen, and in the 1920s had formed 'Jim Mac's Band'. Dominating the living room . . . was an upright piano. . . . As a child, Paul would lie on the floor listening to his father playing 'Stairway to Paradise' and other popular show tunes. [Paul] was sent to have piano lessons, but soon rebelled, preferring to teach himself how to pick out a melody. . . .

In the mid-1950s the BBC had a monopoly of British radio, and as far as it was concerned, pop music meant Frank Sinatra and Vera Lynn. If you wanted to hear the latest American R & B and rock 'n' roll singers, you had to tune to Radio Luxembourg in the evening. To get the boys to go to bed, Jim McCartney rigged up extension cables and headphones from the radio in the living room to their bedrooms.

Through the crackle and hiss . . . they would listen to Elvis, Fats Domino and Little Richard under the sheets."

JOHN MEETS PAUL

When their set was over, the boys moved their equipment into the church's dance hall, where they were to play a second set that evening. With several hours to go, the Quarry Men were sitting around, talking, laughing, and smoking when occasional bass player Ivan Vaughn arrived with a friend. As Shotton writes,

Ivan had thought John might be interested in meeting this guitar-toting friend, who not only was one of the . . . biggest Presley and Little Richard fans, but also knew how to tune his instrument. The [chubby, baby-faced] kid's name, it turned out, was Paul McCartney.[33]

The first meeting between John Lennon and Paul McCartney was rather icy. Lennon was wary of strangers and worried about anybody who might threaten his leadership role. In addition, at fifteen, McCartney was several years younger than Lennon, and with his baby face and puppy-dog eyes he looked even younger. For his part, McCartney was shy, reserved, and a little afraid. He'd seen Lennon around town, but considered him a tough Teddy Boy—someone not to be trifled with.

However, when McCartney began to play piano and sing, relations between the two warmed considerably. McCartney describes the scene:

> John was a little [drunk], leaning over my shoulder, breathing boozily. We were all a little sloshed. I thought, "Bloody hell, who's this?" But he was enjoying what I was playing. "Whole Lotta Shakin' Goin' On". . . and I knew "Tutti Frutti", and "Long Tall Sally". Then I played guitar—upside down [left-handed]. I did "Twenty Flight Rock", *and* knew all the words. The Quarry Men were so knocked out that I actually knew *and* could sing "Twenty Flight Rock".[34]

McCartney further endeared himself to the Quarry Men when he tuned Lennon's guitar. Lennon had not yet learned to tune a guitar and had asked his next-door neighbor to tune it for him. Before the talented McCartney left for the day, he painstakingly wrote out the words to "Twenty Flight Rock" and "Be-Bop-a-Lua" in his neat left-handed script.

Lennon was obviously impressed with McCartney, but there were several reasons why he did not ask him to join the band immediately. The most obvious reason was that McCartney seemed much too talented to join a loud, out-of-tune, disorganized band who had just played their first gig. And more important, Lennon realized that

the young upstart could easily threaten his stature as the group's leader.

"PAUL TOLD ME THE CHORDS"

After their initial meeting, Lennon indicated to Shotton that he wouldn't mind having McCartney in the band. Two weeks passed, however, before Shotton ran into McCartney—as the younger man was riding his bicycle through the neighborhood. When Shotton asked him to join the Quarry Men, McCartney thought about it for more than a minute before answering, "Oh, all right,"[35] and pedaling off on his bicycle.

Shortly after, Shotton's career in the Quarry Men ended abruptly while the group was playing at a party. Everybody in the group was drunk and Lennon, eager to impress some bystanders, grabbed Shotton's glass washboard and smashed it over his head. Shotton remembers,

> It didn't hurt me. I just sat there framed by the washboard, with tears of laughter running down my face. I'd known for a long time that I was no good at music—I was only in the group through being a mate of John's. I was finished with playing, but I didn't want to say so, nor did John. This way let me out and it let John out.[36]

With Shotton gone, Lennon began to spend most of his waking hours at McCartney's house practicing guitar, learning songs, and making big plans for the future.

Except for the music they shared, however, the two could not have been more different. McCartney was studious, respectful of his elders, and careful with his money. Lennon, on the other hand, was a cynical, sharp-tongued, nonconformist who constantly rebelled against authority and would gladly spend his last few pounds on beer.

Fortunately McCartney possessed the patience and respect to teach the Quarry Men's leader how to play guitar properly. As Lennon tells it,

> I could only play the mouth organ and two chords on a guitar when we met. I tuned the guitar like a banjo, so my guitar only had five strings on it. (Paul taught me how to play properly—but I had to learn the chords left-handed, because Paul is left-handed. So I learnt them upside down, and I'd go home and reverse them.) . . . Paul told me the chords I had been playing weren't real chords—and his dad said they weren't even banjo chords.[37]

In addition to learning chords upside down and backwards, Lennon was also hampered by his extremely poor eyesight. The vain musician refused to wear glasses in public and often had to watch McCartney's hands from only inches away.

BOOKED AT THE CAVERN

Although Lennon may have enjoyed McCartney's company, the rest of the Quarry Men did not. They thought that the younger boy was self-centered and resented it when he told them how to play their instruments.

Nonetheless, the group continued to become more professional. They purchased matching stage outfits consisting of black pants, skinny "shoestring" ties, white sports jackets, and white cowboy shirts with fringe. Whalley continued to book them at church dances and dance halls. The latter were often populated with tough Teddy Boys who harassed the band. As Lennon recalled,

An English Teddy Boy. The Quarry Men often played at dance halls, where Teddy Boys would harrass bands.

[The] Teddy boys didn't like you, because all the girls would be watching the group. . . . Afterwards the guys would try and kill you, so most of [the time] was spent running away from people with a guitar under your arm. They'd always catch the drummer; he had all the equipment.[38]

These troubles inspired the Quarry Men's manager to try to book the band at better clubs. By this time Whalley was an apprentice golf professional at a local golf course. A doctor he met at the course had recently opened up a jazz club called the Cavern in the dank brick basement of a downtown Liverpool warehouse. Although the club usually featured jazz, it also booked the occasional skiffle band. Rock music, however, was strictly forbidden. When the Quarry Men played their first gig there and started playing Elvis Presley songs, they were booed by the audience.

ART AND MUSIC

After graduating from Quarry Bank, Lennon began attending the Liverpool College of Art in September 1957. In England, art college was traditionally a place where wayward students were sent to learn some sort of useful graphic arts career. (Although Lennon was the first, many English rock superstars attended art college, including David Bowie, Keith Richards of the Rolling Stones, and members of bands like the Who, the Yardbirds, and the Kinks.)

With the rules, regulations, and dress codes of high school behind him, Lennon stood out at college because of his scruffy looks and bad boy attitude. And unlike his all-male high school, Lennon's college was teeming with artistic and pretty young ladies.

One of those students was Cynthia Powell, a respectable, middle-class girl from one of Liverpool's best neighborhoods. Like Paul McCartney, Cynthia could not have been more different from John Lennon. She was polite, well spoken, and shy. Despite these differences, Lennon and Powell quickly fell in love. And as is the case with many insecure men, Lennon was overpoweringly possessive about his new girlfriend. If Powell so much as looked at another man, Lennon would react with anger.

John Lennon met other students at college as well, including Stuart Sutcliffe, a quiet intellectual whose extraordinary artistic talent was the talk of the school. Lennon and Sutcliffe became instant friends, and the two shared a consuming love for art, Teddy Boy fashion, and, of course, rock and roll.

Although Sutcliffe had little interest in playing in a band, when he sold one of his paintings for £60 (a huge sum at the time), Lennon talked him into spending the entire amount on an electric bass guitar. With this purchase, Sutcliffe became the newest member of Lennon's band.

Coincidentally, the Liverpool College of Art was located just around the corner from Liverpool Institute, McCartney's high school. During his lunch breaks, McCartney often walked over to the college, guitar in hand, and practiced in an unused classroom with Sutcliffe and Lennon.

Occasionally McCartney would bring another guitarist, George Harrison, who was only fourteen. As a college student,

Stuart Sutcliffe, a talented artist and college friend of Lennon, became a member of the Quarry Men when he bought an electric bass guitar.

Lennon was tempted to ignore Harrison, but the young man was a talented guitar player who knew many chords that the others did not. He also dressed in the most flamboyant Teddy Boy fashion, with pink shirts and extremely pointy-toed shoes known as winklepickers.

LOSING JULIA AGAIN

With his band beginning to jell, a respectable outlet for his artistic expression, and Cynthia Powell at his side, Lennon was finally realizing some long-delayed happiness. He was often able to share his exciting

new life with Julia, the two having grown closer than ever. As Coleman writes, "She was more of a friend than a mother-figure, and had an infectious sense of fun. Julia loved music and wanted to know every move John and the Quarry Men were making."[39]

On a July night in 1958, Julia went to visit her sister; Lennon waited at his mother's house for her to return home. While waiting at the bus stop near Mimi's, however, Julia was run down and killed by an off-duty policeman who was driving drunk.

Once again, Lennon's dream of a happy life was shattered. The pain of this experience would remain with him the rest of his life. He talked about it later, saying,

> It was the worst thing that ever happened to me. We'd caught up so much, me and Julia, in just a few years. We could communicate. . . . She was great.
> . . .
>
> That was another big trauma for me. I lost her twice. Once when I moved in with my auntie. And once again at seventeen when she [Julia] actually, physically died. That was very traumatic for me. That was really a hard time for me. It made me very, very bitter. The underlying chip on my shoulder . . . got really big then.[40]

In the months after his mother's death, Lennon drowned his sorrows in alcohol, drinking heavily for the first time in his life and often attending class drunk. Drinking only made the bitter Lennon more aggressive, and the unhappy musician verbally abused others at bars or got into fistfights at parties.

GEORGE HARRISON

When George Harrison joined Lennon and McCartney in the Quarry Men, the main lineup for what would become the Beatles was in place. The Artist Direct website's "George Harrison Biography" (http://ubl.artistdirect. com/fp2.asp?layout=a_b io&artistid=002254) describes the guitarist's early years.

"Harrison was the one Beatle whose upbringing was cushioned by a traditional nuclear family—while his bandmates suffered broken homes and deaths in the family (both John and Paul lost their mums early on), Harrison was raised by a large, close-knit clan of modest means . . . not far from John and Paul's homes. Childhood conferred upon him a sweet-natured disposition that only partially gave way to ire and indifference in his preteen years. Harrison first expressed his hostility to his . . . schoolmasters by dressing in outlandish outfits and sleeping in class, but by the age of thirteen, he had discovered a far better way to channel his anger: playing guitar. George took a liking to skiffle music . . . an appreciation he shared with a cherub-faced chum from the Liverpool Institute named Paul McCartney. The two also found they shared an interest in American rock-and-roll music.

McCartney had the good fortune to join up with . . . the Quarry Men that included another schoolmate, John Lennon, and Harrison joined the group under McCartney's auspices the following year, in 1958. George was sufficiently inspired by the group's success to drop out of the Liverpool Institute to pursue his rock-and-roll dream more earnestly, working as an electrician's apprentice to pay his living expenses (he soon quit because he kept blowing things up). Considerably younger than the rest of the boys, George nevertheless overcame his insecurity and proved himself to be an adept and inventive guitarist."

After a few months, however, Lennon reduced his alcohol intake and returned to music. The pain of his loss had also caused his love for Cynthia to intensify, much to the chagrin of Powell's ultra-conservative mother. Thus, utilizing the power of music and love, Lennon moved beyond the tragedy.

THE SILVER BEETLES

In 1959 Lennon moved out of Mimi's house and into a rundown, one-room apartment with Sutcliffe. The two musicians spent their time hanging around a nearby coffee bar called the Jacaranda run by Allan Williams, who let the Quarry Men play an occasional gig there. Williams also used his influence to book the band in a few other clubs around town.

Since they were performing more, Lennon decided it was time to change the band's name. He wanted to be a rock and roller and believed the name "Quarry Men" sounded too much like a skiffle band. After using the name "Johnny and the Moondogs" for a single gig, the boys decided to emulate the insect-based name of one of their favorite bands, Buddy Holly and the Crickets. Sutcliffe came up with the "Beetles." After that, the band used the name the "Silver Beetles."

Buddy Holly (pictured) and his band, the Crickets, inspired the Quarry Men to change their name to the Silver Beetles, and later, the Beatles.

With John, Paul, and George playing guitars, and Sutcliffe on bass, the Silver Beetles performed with a series of drummers. By 1960, Tommy Moore, a thirty-six-year-old fork-lift driver, served as the regular drummer. His years of experience tightened up the Silver Beetles' sound.

Meanwhile, Allan Williams booked the group at the Jacaranda and another club he owned. Williams even talked a well-known London rock producer, Larry Parnes, into auditioning the Silver Beetles for a Liverpool contest in which the winner would go on a national tour opening for the rising pop star Billy Fury. (Parnes had made a name for himself finding singers to imitate Elvis Presley, cleaning up their acts so that they wouldn't offend the British middle class, and giving them ridiculous stage names such as Vince Eager, Duffy Power, Johnny Gentle, and Dickie Pride.)

The Silver Beetles did not win the contest, but Parnes offered them £18 to warm up for Johnny Gentle on his week-long tour of northern Scotland. Although the band enjoyed hotels, train travel, and for the first time, autograph seekers, all was not well.

Sutcliffe, who had joined the band only because of Lennon's insistence, could barely play his bass guitar. And Moore, who was nearly twice Lennon's age, could not stand the younger man's constant criticism of his playing. When the band returned to Liverpool, Moore quit immediately. Meanwhile, Lennon's aunt Mimi began constantly harassing the young man to put down his guitar and improve his near-failing grades at art college.

But Lennon could not get over his first taste of the rock 'n' roll lifestyle. Instead of worrying about college, he pressured Williams to get the band more gigs. Lennon wanted to play every night as he had during his short tour with Johnny Gentle. Williams was happy to oblige. The Silver Beetles were attracting a growing audience and outselling other acts who played at the Jacaranda. Taking a small percentage of their pay, Williams began to book the band at as many local clubs and ballrooms as possible. The band, however, experienced one more name change. Lennon, using his love of puns, added the word *beat* to the name and dropped the *Silver*, and the band finally became the Beatles.

The Hamburg Experience

While the Beatles made the nightly rounds of the toughest Teddy Boy dance clubs in

The Beatles played their first German gig at the Kaiserkeller in the Reeperbahn (pictured), the notorious red-light district in Hamburg.

Liverpool, making about £10 a night, one of Williams's other bands managed to book themselves in Hamburg, Germany. The band quickly sent Williams a letter, telling him of the great opportunities in Hamburg for English rock bands.

Williams traveled to Hamburg and visited an area known as the Reeperbahn, a notorious red-light district filled with flashing neon signs, music clubs, live sex shows, prostitutes, transvestites, and drunken sailors. The Englishman managed to book the Beatles at the Kaiserkeller for the princely sum of £100 a week beginning in September 1960.

When Lennon heard the news, he was glad to quit art college and begin the life of a traveling musician. Although Mimi advised against it, there was little she could do—her nephew was nineteen years old. One last problem had to be solved, however. The Beatles had no steady drummer.

The band had performed several gigs with Pete Best, the son of Mona Best, owner of the Casbah, a club where the Beatles had played more than 120 gigs. Although he couldn't play very well, the boys asked Best to join the group, and he accepted. On August 16, the Beatles landed in Hamburg. They had no idea what was in store for them, but in their innocence and naiveté they were ready to conquer the world.

3 Becoming a Star

John Lennon may have been one of Liverpool's more notorious teenage delinquents, but when the Beatles landed in Hamburg, Germany, in August 1960, he was, as he later sang, a "nowhere man." When the band first started playing at the Kaiserkeller Club, their musical and stage antics were roundly ignored by the gathered drunks who were there to consume liquor, pick up prostitutes, and get into bloody fights.

For their part, the Beatles were playing eight hours a night, seven days a week, so they had little choice but to experiment with new chords and learn new songs. And as their musicianship improved, their stage antics got wilder. Shotton describes the situation:

> [The] Beatles had to go the extra mile to grab their audience's attention—or, as the Germans put it to *mak schau* [make show]. In John's case, this led to gross impersonations, not only of his favorite rock & roll stars . . . but also of more anonymous cripples and spastics, and even Germany's late Führer [Adolf Hitler]. *"Seig Heil!"* he would shout. "Wake up all you . . . Nazis!" He was even known to appear on stage in his undershorts, sup-

plemented only by a toilet seat worn around his neck.[41]

CHANGING FASHION

Lennon's manic behavior was fueled by amphetamines known as Preludin, or "Prellies," which the band had begun taking every day in order to keep up with their grueling schedule. Coupled with the nonstop flow of strong German beer provided by fans, Lennon was in a haze during much of the time he spent in Hamburg.

Despite Lennon's often insulting and egotistical stage behavior, the Beatles slowly began to build an audience beyond the drunks, transvestites, gangsters, and prostitutes who were regulars at the Kaiserkeller. Young European beatniks and artists had also discovered the Beatles.

One person in particular, Astrid Kirchherr, would have a long-standing influence on the group. Kirchherr was an artist, photographer, and fashion designer—and a spiritual soulmate to the artistic Sutcliffe, with whom she began a love affair. Kirchherr used her camera to record some of the earliest images of the Beatles as a group.

And she talked Sutcliffe into abandoning his greasy Teddy Boy pompadour in favor of the "French cut" hairstyle, later known as the shaggy "moptop" Beatles haircut.

The rest of the Beatles were less than impressed with Sutcliffe's new hairdo, however. Kirchherr describes Lennon's reaction:

> John collapsed laughing. . . . He didn't have the guts to say, "Hey, that looks great", which is what he really thought. John was a complicated person when it came to showing his feelings like that: he hid his emotions. Because he could not bring himself to say what he really thought, he would cover it up and in doing that he would hurt people.[42]

Despite Lennon's initial reaction, he eventually adopted Kirchherr's hairstyle—and by 1965 so would millions of other young men across the globe.

The glory days in Hamburg did not last long. In November 1960 the Beatles played at the Top Ten Club, a direct competitor of

---

SLEEPING IN THE CINEMA

Bruno Koschmider, who owned the clubs where the Beatles played in Hamburg, Germany, was a tough ex-Nazi with a pronounced limp from a war wound. When the Beatles played at his clubs, Koschmider housed them behind the screen at the Bambi Kino, a broken-down old movie theater that he owned. The Beatles describe their primitive accommodations in The Beatles Anthology:

"PAUL: We lived backstage in the Bambi Kino, next to the toilets, and you could always smell them. The room had been an old storeroom, and there were just concrete walls and nothing else. No heat, no wallpaper, not a lick of paint; and two sets of bunk beds, like little camp beds, with not very many covers. We were frozen.

JOHN: We were put in this pigsty, like a toilet it was, in a cinema, a rundown sort of fleapit. *We were living in a toilet,* like right next to the ladies' toilet. We would go to bed late and be woken up the next day by the sound of the cinema show. We'd try to get into the ladies' [bathroom] first, which was the cleanest of the cinema's lavatories, but fat old German women would push past us. . . . That was where we washed. That was our bathroom. It was a bit of a shock in a way.

GEORGE: I never used to shower. There was a washbasin in the lavatory at the Bambi Kino, but there was a limit as to how much of yourself you could wash in it. We could clean our teeth or have a shave, but not much else. . . . I don't think we bathed or showered at all when we were first there."

GROWING POPULARITY

After playing fifty-six hours a week for more than three months in Hamburg, Germany, the Beatles returned to Liverpool. When they began playing their old haunts, such as the Casbah club, they discovered something they hadn't noticed while in their drunken Hamburg haze: Those endless nights onstage had paid off. The Beatles had become a tight, experienced rock 'n' roll band, and word of their new sound spread quickly through the burgeoning Liverpool rock scene.

After performing for large crowds around town, the band returned to Hamburg in April 1961, Harrison having turned eighteen since he was deported. Around this time, Sutcliffe dropped out of the band to pursue art and marry Astrid Kirchherr. Meanwhile, McCartney had taken over Sutcliffe's role as the Beatles' bass player.

On their second tour of Hamburg, the Beatles received an offer from Tony Sheridan, a rising British pop star, to act as a backup band during some recording sessions. As Sheridan sang, the band played "My Bonnie (Lies over the Ocean)," "Ain't She Sweet," "Sweet Georgia Brown," and other standards. When the single of "My Bonnie (Lies over the Ocean)" was released under the name "Tony Sheridan and the Beat Brothers," it sold a respectable 180,000 copies in Germany. The single was also released in Britain under the name "Tony Sheridan and the Beatles" but did not sell as well.

Upon returning to Liverpool, the Beatles were hired to play daily lunch-hour shows at the Cavern, where they had played ear-

In 1960, the Beatles played at the Top Ten Club, a move that offered more money. The Kaiserkeller's owner vengefully had Harrison, Best, and McCartney deported for playing at his competitor's club.

the Kaiserkeller, because that club's owner offered them more money than they made at the Kaiserkeller. Seeking revenge, Bruno Koschmider, the owner of the Kaiserkeller, notified Hamburg police that George Harrison was only seventeen years old. Harrison was quickly deported back to Liverpool and the Beatles carried on without him. Days later, however, Pete Best and Paul McCartney were both arrested and deported on phony arson charges filed by Koschmider. Without a band, Lennon was left to drift back to Liverpool, penniless and alone, carrying his new Rickenbacker guitar on his back. Within days of returning home, however, John Lennon was ready to rock again.

lier to jazz audiences who did not appreciate their rock music. Now rock was king in Liverpool and the Cavern had dropped its jazz acts. And among all of Liverpool's thriving rock bands, the Beatles were drawing the largest crowds.

Since fourteen-year-old girls, office workers, and secretaries with short skirts and beehive hairdos began to pack into the club at noon, the Beatles were also given night bookings at the Cavern. Over the next two years, the band would go on to play 292 shows at the club.

To enter the Cavern, patrons had to walk down eighteen stone steps that led from the bright, busy streets of downtown Liverpool into a windowless basement packed wall to wall with sweaty dancers. The club actually

THE FIRST RECORDING SESSION

In April 1961, the Beatles were recruited by Tony Sheridan to record some songs for Polydor Records in Hamburg. Frank Daniels describes Sheridan and his relationship with the Beatles on his "Across the Universe" website (www.scs.unr.edu/~fd aniels/stuff/tony.htm).

"By age 18, Tony [Sheridan] was playing guitar on British TV—being the first musician *allowed* to play electric guitar there. By 1960, he was backing Eddie Cochran [a top-selling artist of the time]. Sheridan came close to acquiring a recording contract in England, but never quite made it there. So when he was asked to play rock and roll music at one of the clubs in Germany, he jumped at the chance. By mid-1960, Tony Sheridan and the Jets were playing at the Kaiserkeller in Hamburg.

Not long after, Tony graduated to the Top Ten Club, when he met the Beatles and other British bands who were by then playing in Germany. It was during this period that Sheridan took a young George Harrison under his wing and helped him better master the guitar. George was very eager to learn, and by the time of the Beatles' second trip to Hamburg, the Beatles and Tony Sheridan had become accustomed to playing together.

By that time, too, Polydor Records was seeking to offer Tony his first recording contract. Since Tony often played with the Beatles, they were familiar with the songs he might record. . . .

As to what was recorded, it is known for certain that 'My Bonnie (Lies Over the Ocean),' 'The Saints (When the Saints Go Marching In),' 'Why,' 'Cry For a Shadow,' 'Ain't She Sweet,' 'Take Out Some Insurance On Me Baby,' and 'Nobody's Child' were recorded at that (first) session."

consisted of three intersecting underground tunnels where there was no ventilation, everyone was smoking, and the brick walls oozed foul brown water that dripped from the gutters above. A small stage was constructed at the end of one of the tunnels, and the music from the bands ricocheted off the walls like gunfire. For John Lennon this was heaven. Shotton, who was a frequent guest at the Cavern, describes their shows:

> Unlike other local bands who played the Cavern, the Beatles studiously avoided anything that smacked of show-biz, or even professionalism in the usual sense of the word. Rather than follow a rehearsed programme, they preferred simply to launch into whichever titles members of the band—or the audience—happened to call out that day. John, with his lifelong inability to remember lyrics, often ended up ad-libbing the words to his favorite rock & roll classics, peppering the familiar melody with obscenities, in-jokes, and snatches of his inimitable gobbledegook. As often as not, the results singularly failed to fit the song's original meter, and the Beatles' rendition would peter out in a chorus of laughter. John, Paul, and George also persisted in smoking and chewing [tobacco] throughout their sets,

The Beatles rest onstage at the Cavern. The band played 292 shows at the crowded, smoky underground club.

and even took their cheese roll lunches onstage. This evident spontaneity—coupled with the awesome firepower and tightness of the band when it did get down to business—perfectly complemented the primeval ambience of the place itself, and enabled the Beatles to regularly eclipse all other . . . bands who preceded or followed them onto the Cavern stage.[43]

MEETING A MANAGER

The Beatles were quickly developing a large following, but not all of their followers were teenagers and young people on their lunch breaks. One of their oldest fans at that time was twenty-seven-year-old Brian Epstein whose family owned a record shop called the NEMS (North End Music Store) a few doors down from the Cavern.

Epstein first heard about the Beatles when a fan walked into the NEMS on October 28, 1961, and asked for a copy of "My Bonnie" by Tony Sheridan and the Beatles. Epstein tried to satisfy every customer's request, so the prim and proper store owner ventured into the Cavern, which he described in his autobiography as "black as a deep grave, dank and damp and smelly,"[44] to ask the band where he could find the record.

What Epstein found in the foul Cavern Club was a room packed with excited teenagers swooning over four unkempt, unprofessional musicians who were laughing, talking, pretending to hit each other, and playing with their backs to the audience. As a good businessman, Epstein couldn't help but notice that many girls were carrying large purses with homemade embroidered messages that read "I Love You John," "I Love Paul," and "I Love the Beatles."[45] And Epstein was mesmerized by the band, writing, "[They] gave a captivating and honest show and they had very considerable magnetism. I loved their ad libs and I was fascinated by this, to me, new music with its pounding bass beat in its vast and engulfing sound. There was quite clearly an excitement in the otherwise unpleasant dungeon."[46]

When Epstein introduced himself to the band, they were wary of the respectable, upper-class gentleman in a tailored suit with stilted mannerisms. Lennon said, "He looked efficient and rich, that's all I remember."[47] In spite of the great social gulf between Epstein and the band, when he met with the group a week later and offered to be their manager, Lennon immediately agreed. For his fee, Epstein asked for 25 percent of the band's earnings, which was a good deal during a time when most managers took 50 percent.

Epstein quickly set about persuading the Beatles to clean up their act. He asked them to wear suits, shirts, and ties and to stop eating, swearing, and smoking onstage. As Lennon commented,

> [He] said our look wasn't right, we'd never get past the door at a good place. . . . It was a choice of making it or still eating chicken on stage. We respected his views. We stopped champing at cheese rolls . . . paid a lot more attention to what we're doing, did our best to be on time and we smartened up.[48]

LENNON'S HISTORY OF THE BEATLES

In the 1960s, Liverpool rock bands were featured in a magazine called Mercy Beat. *The editor of the magazine greatly appreciated John Lennon's poetry and short stories and asked him to write a column for the paper. Lennon's first published work, excerpted here from Ray Coleman's book,* Lennon, *was a nonsensical history of the Beatles written in typical Lennon style with exaggerations, puns, and hilariously misused words.*

"Being a Short Diversion on the Dubious Origins of Beatles Translated from John Lennon.

Once upon a time there were three little boys called John, George and Paul. . . . They decided to get together because they were the getting together type. When they were together they wondered what for after all, what for? So all of a sudden they all grew guitars and fashioned a noise. Funnily enough, no one was interested, least of all the three little men. So-o-o on discovering a fourth even littler man called Stuart Sutcliffe running about them they said, quote 'Sonny get a bass guitar and you will be alright' and he did—but he wasn't alright because he couldn't play it. So they sat on him with comfort 'til he could play. Still, there was no beat, and a kindly old man said, quote 'Thou hast not drums!' We had no drums! they coffed. So a series of drums came and went and came. . . .

Many people ask what are the Beatles? Why Beatles? Ugh, Beatles how did the name arrive. So we will tell you. It came in a vision—a man appeared on a flaming pie and said unto them 'From this day on you are Beatles with an A.' Thank you, Mister Man, they said, thanking him."

Epstein also worked tirelessly to promote the Beatles. He called on his many connections in the press and the music business to give publicity to the band, and he persuaded the management at the Cavern to double the amount it was paying the Beatles. He also booked the Beatles into a steady stream of nicer clubs where they were paid better than ever before.

When the band wasn't playing, Lennon spent many long hours with Epstein plotting and planning the Beatles' future. The Beatles' manager was not shy about his appreciation for the band—especially Lennon. As his brother Clive Epstein stated,

> Brian told me privately he believed John was a genius and of course he assured . . . me that they would be bigger than Elvis Presley. . . . Brian was definitely closer to John than the others; there was a mental contact between them that was perfect and really vital for the group's future.[49]

Losing Sutcliffe

With the benefit of Epstein's careful planning, the Beatles planned to return to Hamburg in style on April 13, 1962. They had traveled in broken-down vans, trains, or ferries before, but Epstein provided first-class airfare. And on this trip, the Beatles were booked at the prestigious Star-Club, a much more respectable venue than the low-class Kaiserkeller.

Throughout this period, Lennon had continued to exchange letters with Sutcliffe and had learned that his friend suffered from paralyzing headaches. But Lennon and others were stunned when Sutcliffe died of a brain hemorrhage in Hamburg on April 10, three days before the Beatles were to return. When Kirschherr met Lennon at the airport to tell him the bad news, she said, "He went into this hysterical laughter, and couldn't stop. It was his way of not

As the Beatles' manager, Brian Epstein persuaded the band to clean up their act. He and Lennon spent many hours together planning the Beatles' future.

wanting to face the truth. John went deep in to himself for just a little while after the news. . . . I knew that he and Stuart genuinely loved each other."[50]

A RECORD CONTRACT

Back in Liverpool, the band continued to play while Epstein attempted to get them a recording contract in London, where sophisticated record producers were less than impressed. Before long, the Beatles were rejected by every major label. Most executives argued that they did not think there was a future in rock and roll. As Lennon recalled, "Even in Hamburg when we auditioned for those German companies they would tell us to stop playing the rock and the blues and concentrate on the other stuff [such as ballads and cabaret songs] because they all thought rock was dead."[51] After the Beatles became a smash success, however, the words of Dick Rowe, head of Decca Records, came back to haunt him and others. He said, "Guitar groups are on their way out, Mr. Epstein."[52]

Despite Rowe's pessimism, Epstein refused to give up. He traveled to London more than twenty times attempting to secure a record deal for the band. Each time he returned unsuccessful, he was afraid to tell the band since without a recording contract, the Beatles felt that there was little reason to continue as a group.

Meanwhile, the band began to write their own songs. Lennon and McCartney were a particularly potent songwriting team, and early songs such as "Love Me Do," "PS I Love You," and "Ask Me Why" were excellent vehicles for showcasing the band's tight vocal harmonies and instrumental talent during live performances.

In August 1962, Epstein's dogged determination finally paid off. The Beatles were awarded a contract with Parlophone Records, a subsidiary of the prestigious EMI record company. Parlophone's in-house producer was George Martin, a classically trained pianist whose background was producing light orchestral music. Fortunately for the Beatles, Martin had also produced several over-the-top comedy records for a group known as the Goon Show. When it came time to work with the joking, mocking, and sarcastic Lennon, Martin would feel right at home.

"RINGO NEVER, PETE BEST FOREVER!"

Upon hearing the news of the contract, the Beatles immediately traveled to London and recorded "Love Me Do," featuring Lennon's unique harmonica playing. Martin, however, found one serious problem with the Beatles' music: Pete Best's plodding drumming, which had been a bane to the group for years, was not up to professional standards. The rest of the band didn't have the heart to tell their friend and left it up to Epstein to fire the hapless drummer.

For his replacement, the Beatles set their sights on Ringo Starr, who had sat in with the group on several occasions. Having been a steady member of the popular group Rory Storm and the Hurricanes for several years, Ringo, whose real name was Richard Starkey, was considered to be the greatest drummer in Liverpool. As Lennon said,

George Martin, house producer at Parlophone Records, gave the Beatles their first recording contract in 1962. Martin encouraged the band to replace drummer Pete Best.

"We knew of Ringo. Ringo was a star in his own right before we even met. Ringo was a professional drummer, sang and performed, so his talents would have come out one way or the other."[53]

Not everyone was so enamored with Starr, however. Although Pete Best had difficulty keeping time, his movie-star good looks had made him one of the most popular members of the band with teenage girls. During Starr's first gig at the Cavern, the mob turned violent and began to chant "Pete is best!" and "Ringo never, Pete Best forever!"[54] In the melee that followed, Harrison was given a black eye by an angry teen.

MARRIAGE VOWS

On August 23, 1962, one week after Starr joined the Beatles, John Lennon finally married Cynthia Powell, who was now pregnant. As Shotton wrote, "In those days if you got your girlfriend pregnant, you married her, and that was that."[55] The two were married in

RINGO'S EARLY LIFE

The Ringo Home Page (http://web2.airmail. net/gshultz/bio1.html) by Gary Shultz features a biography of Ringo Starr's life before the Beatles.

"Ringo Starr was born on July seventh, 1940. Named after his father, he was the only child of Richard Starkey and Elsie Gleave. . . . Richard Sr. left home when little Richard, now called Ritchie, was three. . . .

At the age of five, Ritchie started school . . . but his school career hit the first of many snags when, at age six, he developed appendicitis. His appendix ruptured resulting in peritonitis and a ten week coma. Elsie was told on several occasions that her boy would not live, but eventually, to the doctor's surprise, he came round and slowly began to mend. . . . When he was finally released, Ritchie found that he was very behind in his school work. He couldn't read or write, so a neighbor child . . . was recruited to help teach him. . . .

In 1953 . . . Ritchie developed pleurisy. Complications resulted in another hospitalization, this one lasting two years. . . . When he emerged from the hospital at fifteen, he knew that returning to school was out of the question. . . .

In December of 1957, [Ritchie got] his first real set of drums. . . . In November of 1959 Ritchie officially joined . . . Rory Storm and the Hurricanes. . . .

Ever the showman, Rory . . . suggested that Ritchie adopt a flashier stage monicker [name]. Because of his penchant for wearing rings on his fingers, Ritchie naturally evolved into "Rings" and then quickly [evolved] into the more Western sounding "Ringo." Starkey became shortened to Starr because it fit better with Ringo. . . .

Ringo eagerly threw in his lot with the Beatles, playing with them for the first time as their official drummer on August 18, 1962, a mere eighteen days before their scheduled recording session for EMI at Abbey Road."

Seen here in Ringo's boyhood bedroom are photographs of him with his mother (left), Ringo (center), and Ringo's father.

a short ceremony with only McCartney, Harrison, Epstein, and a few others present. Since Lennon's aunt Mimi did not approve of the "scandalous" circumstances of the marriage, the couple moved in together at an extra apartment Epstein owned. Lennon would keep his marriage a secret. The Beatles were afraid that as a married man, teenage fans would be less inclined to worshipfully adore John Lennon. And judging from Lennon's comments, it was obvious he was not exactly thrilled with the marriage:

> I thought it would be goodbye to the group, getting married. None of us ever took girls to the Cavern as we thought we would lose fans . . . [and] I did feel embarrassed, walking about married. It was like walking about with odd socks on or your flies open.[56]

Lennon's marriage would remain a guarded secret until the mid-1960s.

To the Top of the Charts

By the autumn of 1962, "Love Me Do" was selling briskly in Liverpool, putting the Beatles' first single in the British Top 20. Martin suggested that the Beatles follow their hit with a tune written by a professional songwriter. At that time many major rock stars, including Elvis Presley, did not write their own material, instead relying on sure-fire hits from professional tunesmiths. Lennon, however, refused, insisting that the Beatles had plenty of original material to choose from.

Martin conceded to Lennon's demands, and the Beatles recorded two Lennon/McCartney compositions, "Please Please Me" and "From Me to You." Both rocketed to number one within days of their release. These hit singles were later included on the Beatles' first long-playing (LP) album, *Please Please Me,* recorded in a marathon ten-hour session on February 11, 1963.

The fourteen songs on *Please Please Me* were a combination of original and cover songs (songs written by other people) that had been the core of the Beatles' stage act for several years. The band's talent is well displayed on the album. Rock songs such as "I Saw Her Standing There" demonstrate the group's penchant for soaring three-part harmony, while "Do You Want to Know a Secret?" shows that the group can put forth songs that even parents could love.

Upon its release, *Please Please Me* immediately went to the top of the LP charts, staying there a record-breaking twenty-nine weeks. Little more than a year after meeting Brian Epstein, the Beatles were the hottest act in the British Isles.

"Yeah, Yeah, Yeah"

With fame came fans. The Beatles toured Great Britain relentlessly from southern England to Wales and northern Scotland. Wherever they went, "Beatle hysteria" was breaking out all over. Concerts sold out so fast that, to obtain tickets, fans camped out two to three days in advance outside of box offices.

When the band's fourth single, "She Loves You," was released in August 1963, the "yeah, yeah, yeah" chorus had millions of people singing along with the "Fab

Four." By this time, nearly every schoolboy in Britain was growing his hair long in the fashion of John, Paul, George, and Ringo. Stores that sold pointy ankle-high boots with stacked heels, or "Beatle boots," could not keep them in stock. The Teddy Boy look was officially dead, ironically killed by John Lennon, one of its greatest fans. Now, millions of British boys were imitating their new heroes, a group of scruffy young lads from Liverpool.

Lennon, the angry young man with a chip on his shoulder, seemed to be changed by his newfound fame. Of all the members of the group, he was the most diligent about signing autographs for the growing legion of fans who stood around stage doors and hotel lobbies. The drug and alcohol binges from the Hamburg days were replaced by sodas, milk, and pack after pack of cigarettes. As singer Kenny Lynch recalled, "[They] were getting the kicks just from performing and making such a quick impact on audiences all over England. They didn't need any false effects from drugs."[57]

Free from drugs and temporarily relieved from his emotional pain, Lennon became a prolific songwriter, jotting down lyrics on napkins, cigarette packs, and scraps of paper. He wrote on the tour bus, in hotel lobbies, and in backstage dressing rooms.

As hit after hit topped the charts, the Beatles embarked on four long tours all over Britain. While the twenty-two-year-old Lennon was driving from one town to the next playing to sold-out crowds, Cynthia had a baby. John Charles Julian Lennon was born on April 8, 1963.

Like Fred Lennon, John was absent when Julian, as he was called, came into the world. Unlike his father, however, Lennon arrived three days later and was absolutely thrilled at the sight of his newborn son. By November, Lennon was able to afford an expensive mansion in London's exclusive St. George's Hill district. Although he didn't like the restricted upper-class atmosphere of the neighborhood, he thought it would be best for his new wife and son.

John Lennon was quickly becoming a millionaire, and he didn't forget his old friends. During a get-together with Shotton on Christmas 1963, Lennon stuffed a brown envelope in his old friend's pocket. When Shotton opened the envelope the next day, he found Lennon's weekly paycheck— equivalent to around $2,000. (Shotton was earning around $100 a week at the time.) A month later, Lennon gave Shotton $40,000 to open a gambling parlor in Liverpool, saying, "Look Pete, you'd do the same for me wouldn't you?"[58]

"Electricity Generated by John"

Between September and November 1963, "She Loves You" spent six weeks at number one on the British charts, and thirty-three weeks total in the Top 50. In December, "I Want to Hold Your Hand" went to number one for five weeks and spent the next twenty-two weeks on the Top 50. Although it was primarily teenagers who loved the music, adults and the media were also becoming fans, and John Lennon quickly became a clever and humorous representative of the younger generation. As Coleman writes,

This promotional photo shows off the Beatles' new clean-cut look.

One major reason the Beatles were so acceptable to the Old Guard [established press], and even to jazz snobs, was the outspoken style of John Lennon. Quite apart from their records that were pounding up the charts . . . Lennon's acrid interviews became the group's unexpected strength. The music could take care of itself, but the electricity generated by John, more than any of the Fab Four, was so alive that he quickly became the most sought-after Beatle.

Most pop stars before John had had a problem sustaining a conversation beyond the bland talk of their latest record and their narcissism. Lennon single-handedly stood the credo on its head. In his speech alone, pop music grew up. . . . He would talk about anything and everything, he would criticize himself and claim nothing whatsoever for his group.[59]

Although Lennon's modesty played well in the press, in private he was ready to conquer the world—which at that time meant taking America by storm. Lennon would not have to wait for long. On November 22, 1963, U.S. president John F. Kennedy was assassinated in Dallas, Texas. For the next several months, traditional American optimism was marred by depression as people mourned the loss of their handsome young president. Young Americans who had witnessed the tragedy were particularly angered and disillusioned. Thus, by early 1964 they were ready for a positive sound to cheer them up. John Lennon and the Beatles would soon provide the perfect tonic.

Chapter

4 Beatlemania

The early 1960s were not a stellar time for American rock-and-roll music. There was little innovation, and the men who had launched the rock revolution had virtually disappeared. Chuck Berry was arrested in a sex scandal, Elvis Presley was in the army, Little Richard quit playing rock music to become a preacher, and Buddy Holly had died in a 1959 plane crash. The musical void was filled by middle-of-the-road, clean-cut white crooners such as Frankie Avalon, Pat Boone, Bobby Vee, and Bobby Vinton. There was even a popular group of Belgian nuns known as the Singing Nuns.

While the Beatles played songs like "Twist and Shout" and "I Saw Her Standing There" to nearly hysterical British audiences, American teens were served up syrupy sweet ballads such as "Roses Are Red (My Love)," "Hey Paula," and "Blue Velvet." There were a few bright stars on the radio, such as Ray Charles, Roy Orbison, and "girl groups" like the Marvelettes and Chiffons, but in general, the pop music business was in desperate need of a shakeup.

For the average young American, strict conformity was the order of the day. Most teenage males dressed in the manner of the teen idols, wearing penny loafers, cardigan sweaters, and white pin-stripe shirts. Tough boys dressed in black leather jackets, tight blue jeans, and slicked back hair. Almost no American men, except for a few beatniks on the East and West Coasts, had long hair. That was about to change—practically overnight.

"THE BEATLES ARE COMING!"

In the early '60s, New York City was the American entertainment capital, home of national TV, radio, and recording companies. In late 1963, however, almost no one in the United States had heard of the Beatles. Although the group had sold more than 1 million records in England, as Shotton says, "[The] very notion that a British pop star might *ever* 'make it' in the U.S.A. would have seemed preposterous to anyone who wasn't named Brian Epstein or John Lennon."[60]

This was clearly demonstrated to Epstein when EMI's American subsidiary, Capitol Records, refused to release the Beatles' first four singles. One executive commented, "We don't think the Beatles will do anything in [the American] market."[61]

Ignoring the record executive, just as he had ignored shortsighted British studio heads, Epstein flew in to New York City on November 5, 1963, the day after the Beatles performed for Britain's Queen Mother at the annual Royal Command Performance variety show. Epstein met with Capitol's East Coast representative, and the record rep liked the Beatles' as-yet-unreleased single "I Want to Hold Your Hand." Unlike "Love Me Do," "Please Please Me," and "She Loves You," the executive thought this record might sell.

Before he returned to England, Epstein had another stroke of good luck. He was able to book the Beatles on *The Ed Sullivan Show* for two consecutive weekends, February 9 and 16. *The Ed Sullivan Show* was the most popular variety show on TV, and Sullivan's approval of a band could make them an instant success in the United States.

On December 5, when "I Want to Hold Your Hand" was released in Britain, it quickly sold 1 million copies and went to number

In the early 1960s American rock-and-roll music centered around clean-cut white crooners like Frankie Avalon. In 1963, almost no one in the United States had heard of the Beatles.

one. Days later, a disc jockey in Washington, D.C., played a copy of the song that he had picked up overseas. Within minutes the station's phones began ringing off the hook with hundreds of requests for the song to be played again. Other radio stations across the country obtained advance copies of the song from Capitol, and when it was released in the United States on December 25, it sold a million copies within days.

Without setting foot in the United States, the Beatles began generating intense interest in the American press. As Fred Bronson writes in *The Billboard Book of Number One Hits*, "Suddenly, there was a media explosion. *Life, The New York Times*, CBS, the Associated Press and *The Washington Post* all assigned reporters to file stories on the Beatles."[62]

One month later, "She Loves You" was released, and it too went to number one on the Billboard charts, making it the first time any artist had two consecutive chart toppers. By February, the Beatles had become America's hottest band. Their popularity was aided by Capitol Records, which budgeted $50,000 (an enormous sum at the time) for billboards, ads, and flyers that read "The Beatles are Coming!"[63] Meanwhile, *The Ed Sullivan Show* received fifty thousand ticket requests for the Beatles' performance in its seven-hundred-seat theater.

"OUT OF THEIR MINDS"

When the Beatles' airplane landed at New York's Kennedy Airport on February 7,

Thousands of screaming fans greeted the Beatles when their plane landed in New York City in February 1964. The band had no idea that such a huge crowd would welcome them to America.

1964, the band looked out the window and saw five thousand screaming fans. The group had no idea the crowd was there to greet them and thought the president must be arriving at the same time. But the shrieking of the teenage girls overwhelmed them when they stepped off the plane. Lennon recalled the scene: "They're wild; they're all wild. They just all seem out of their minds. I've never seen anything like it in my life. We just walk through it like watching a film. You feel as though it's something that's happening to somebody else."[64]

Two nights later, more than 73 million Americans—almost half the country—watched the Beatles on *The Ed Sullivan Show*. In the following days a new word, *Beatlemania*, was coined to define the near-hysterical adoration generated by John, Paul, George, and Ringo.

Shortly after, the Beatles played their first nontelevised American concert to ten thousand shrieking fans in Washington, D.C., and two concerts at Carnegie Hall, for which 6 million ticket requests were received for the hall's three thousand seats. Though Lennon appreciated the adoration, he found it difficult to play complicated songs with tight harmonies before tens of thousands of hysterical teenage girls:

> It wouldn't matter if I never sang. . . . Often I don't anyway. I just stand there and make mouth movements. Nobody knows. I reckon we can send out four waxworks dummies of ourselves and that would satisfy the crowds. Beatles concerts are [sic]

nothing to do with music. . . . They're just . . . tribal rites.[65]

While fans were scrambling for concert tickets and snapping up millions of Beatles records, Lennon's choice of cover songs reminded Americans of rock music's black roots. Included among the Beatles' clever and melodic originals were songs such as Chuck Berry's "Rock and Roll Music," Smokey Robinson's "You Really Got a Hold on Me," and other tunes by African American singers. Although Elvis and many other white pop stars had recorded black American music, Lennon's soulful vocals were truer to the originals, and the Beatles publicly acknowledged their debt to black recording artists. In this manner, it was said that the Beatles reintroduced black rock and roll to Americans who had forgotten or ignored the African American origins of the popular music.

FAB FOUR FASHION

For the next several years the Beatles engaged in a nonstop whirlwind of concerts, press conferences, TV appearances, and more. All of the top five Billboard best sellers were Beatles songs, and the group had 14 singles in the Top 100. When "Can't Buy Me Love" was about to be released, it garnered 2.1 million advance sales orders, another first.

Meanwhile, much as it had in Britain, American fashion changed practically overnight. Millions of young men bought "Beatle boots" and collarless suit coats, and

Ed Sullivan examines an electric guitar while Epstein and the Beatles look on at The Ed Sullivan Show's *rehearsal. Seventy-three million viewers tuned into the show to see the Beatles perform.*

let their hair grow over their ears and into long bangs. Suddenly, long hair became a symbol of a rebellious attitude, a form of disobedience that enraged older people. Teenage boys with long hair were expelled from school or forced to cut their hair. In some areas, long-haired boys were attacked and beaten. Those who couldn't grow long hair bought "Beatle wigs," which were selling by the thousands.

Epstein also held marketing rights to dozens of other Beatles products, including lunch boxes, trading cards, totebags, clocks, stamps, and other trinkets. The faces of John,

Paul, George, and Ringo were everywhere. Never before had any musical stars been promoted in this manner. In addition, the Beatles were featured on the covers of every major news magazine and in special fan magazines that were published to fill the demand for anything concerning the Beatles.

The Beatles even changed the way people talked. Unlike many British stars who used the proper "Queen's English," the band did not hide their nasal Liverpool accents. Instead, they joyously insisted on using Liverpool slang words, which were widely published in magazines. Words

WOOING THE PRESS

When the Beatles landed in New York in February 1964, a skeptical press was there to meet them, along with five thousand shrieking fans. Although the assembled reporters were prepared to shoot down the long-haired moptops, the Beatles quickly won their hearts and minds with quick wit and humble humor, as Philip Norman reports in Shout.

"The New York press, with a few exceptions, succumbed [to the Beatles' charms] as quickly as the fans. Within minutes, one svelte and sarcastic woman journalist was babbling into a telephone: 'They are absolutely too cute for words. America is going to just love them'. . . . Meanwhile, in the conference room, their one hundred and ninety-eight colleagues continued the interrogation which was supposed to have been ironic and [awkward] but which had produced anything but discomfiture. The Beatles were at their flash-quick, knockabout, impudent best.

In their first American press conference, the Beatles charmed the New York press.

'Are you going to have a haircut while you're in America?' [a reporter asked.]

'We had one yesterday,' John replied.

'Will you sing something for us?'

'We need money first,' John said.

'What's your secret?'

'If we knew that,' George said, 'we'd each form a group and manage it'. . . .

'Are you part of a teenage rebellion against the older generation?'

'It's a dirty lie,' [said Ringo.]

'What do you think of the campaign in Detroit to stamp out the Beatles?'

'We've got a campaign of our own,' Paul said, 'to stamp out Detroit.'"

such as *grotty* for grotesque, *groovy* for good, *gear* for fabulous, and *rave* for party were quickly picked up by American teens.

While the Beatles were turning American culture on its axis, Lennon remained the tough Liverpool Teddy Boy regardless of his lovable "moptop" image. He was offended by the musical compromises he had to make to appeal to the mindless shrieks of the adolescent "Beatlemaniacs." According to Paul's brother Mike McCartney,

> The others didn't have John's resentment of having to do what he was doing to be a Beatle. . . . They thought they were just bloody lucky they were getting away with it for so long. But John always had that drive, something ticking over, the need to do something else. It was: "Ah, so *this* is what we have to do to be bigger than Elvis? OK, let's go, but I'm not going to give one hundred per cent of me." That individuality stayed and marked

him out as the most original of the four.[66]

THE FIRST MUSIC VIDEO

At the time of the Beatles' triumph, there were only three television stations in the United States, and the media as it's known today did not exist. There was no MTV, Internet, twenty-four-hour entertainment networks, or any other way for hungry Beatles fans to stay in touch with the band that they loved. So when the movie *A Hard Day's Night* premiered in June 1964, Beatles fans all over the world were able to get an inside look at their favorite band for the first time.

A Hard Day's Night opened in five hundred American movie theaters and grossed $1.3 million in its first week. More than a business success, the movie certified the Beatles as bona fide movie stars, and added

A Hard Day's Night *was an immediate hit for the Beatles in 1964 and is now considered a classic. The movie established the band members as movie stars and created a bond between the fans and the group.*

IN HIS OWN WRITE

In 1964, when Lennon released In His Own Write, *a book of original short stories, the book quickly became a best-seller. This excerpt, titled "Nicely Nicely Clive," clearly demonstrates Lennon's wacky humor and word-twisting writing style.*

"To Clive Barrow it was just an ordinary day nothing unusual or strange about it, everything quite navel, nothing outstanley just another day but to Roger it was something special, a day amongst days . . . a red lettuce day . . . because Roger was getting married and as he dressed that morning he thought about the gay batchelor soups he'd had with all his pals. And Clive said nothing. To Roger everything was different, wasn't this the day his Mother had told him about, in his best suit and all that, grimming and shakeing hands, people tying boots and ricebudda on his car.

To have and to harm . . . till death duty part . . . be knew it all off by hertz. Clive Barrow seemed oblivious. Roger could visualise Anne in her flowing weddy drag, being wheeled up the aisle, smiling a blessing. He had butterfield in his stomarce as he fastened his bough tie and brushed his hairs."

to their legend. The shots of the Beatles traveling, hanging around backstage, and answering fan mail in hotel rooms also helped moviegoers bond with the band. It was also the first true music video ever filmed, with "jump cuts" of the band leaping through the air, running wildly across empty fields, playing live concerts before screaming audiences, and being chased through London's streets by teenage girls. The movie is now considered a classic, and film critic Roger Ebert even uses *A Hard Day's Night* to teach film classes, analyzing it with his students one shot at a time.

The movie showed that the Beatles were sweet, cute, funny, fashionable, and that they sang like angels. Lennon's irreverent wisecracks and antics demonstrated to fans that they too could rebel against the predictable, stale, and boring. A majority of the teens who watched the movie developed deep feelings of empathy—and love—for John, Paul, George, and Ringo.

Flush with millions of dollars from the success of touring, record sales, and *A Hard Day's Night*, Lennon continued to write prolifically. When not penning clever songs, he scrawled short stories similar to those he wrote when he was in grammar school. These were published in a book called *In His Own Write*. Inspired by *Alice in Wonderland*, Lennon's stories have zany

The Torture of Touring

John Lennon was never one to mince words. In a bitter post-Beatles interview with Rolling Stone *magazine published in 1970 and called* Lennon Remembers, *Lennon recalled the hellish part of being in the world's most popular band.*

"Wherever we went on tour . . . there's always a few seats laid aside for . . . people in wheelchairs. . . . Because we were famous, we were supposed to have [the handicapped] . . . in our dressing room all the time. . . . And it's always the mother or nurse pushing them on you . . . like you were Christ or something, as if there were some aura about you which will rub off on them. . . .

It just built up, the bigger that we got, the more unreality we had to face, the more we were expected to do until when you didn't shake hands with a mayor's wife she starts abusing you and screaming and saying 'How dare they!' . . . [They] were always threatening . . . to make bad publicity about us if we didn't see their bloody daughter with their braces on their teeth. And it was always the police chief's daughter or the Lord Mayor's daughter, all the most obnoxious kids, because they had the most obnoxious parents. . . . Those were the most humiliating experiences. . . . I couldn't take it, it would hurt me, I would go insane, swearing at them, whatever, I'd always do something. I couldn't take it, it was awful, and all that business was awful. It was a . . . humiliation. One has to completely humiliate oneself to be what the Beatles were, and that's what I resent. I mean . . . I didn't foresee; it just happened . . . gradually, until this complete craziness is surrounding you and you're doing exactly what you don't want to do with people you can't stand, the people you hated when you were ten."

titles such as "Partly Dave," "Nicely Nicely Clive," "Liddypool," "Halibut Returb," and "The Fingletoad Resort of Teddiviscious." Like everything else Lennon touched at this time, the silly, sarcastic book was a best-seller, with 100,000 copies sold within weeks of its release. A year later, Lennon published *A Spaniard in the Works*, with similar success.

Concert Hysteria

Beatlemania, however, proved that there might be such a thing as too much love. When the Beatles arrived at San Francisco airport in August 1964 at the beginning of their first full-fledged American tour, they had to be placed directly into a protective iron cage after leaving the airplane. Ravenous crowds lunged at the cage, however, and the terrified band was removed seconds before the cage collapsed under the weight of hundreds of people. For the next month, the Beatles played twenty-three 35-minute shows and traveled more than twenty-two thousand miles across the United States in a private plane. Philip Norman describes the nightmare of touring:

> At times they did not know if they were in Jacksonville, Baltimore, Denver, Cincinnati, Detroit or Atlantic City. Everywhere, there were mayors and senators and senators' wives, and sheriffs and deputies; there were the town's most exclusive call girls; there were crippled children, seated in wheelchairs that were lined up along the stage, and later brought into the Beatles' dressing room as if to see or touch them might work a miracle. From stadium or conference hall, whichever it chanced to be, they would run, in their sodden suits, directly to the aircraft, flying through the night to another sky, another airport, another screaming sea of faces, pressed against police backs or quilted by steel perimeter wire. . . .
>
> At Love Field, Dallas, fans broke through the police barrier, climbed onto the aircraft wings and belabored the windows with Coke bottles. Later, at the hotel, a chambermaid was kidnapped and threatened with a knife unless she revealed the location of the Beatles' suite; other girls had to be rescued from the air-conditioning shaft.

> . . . In Seattle, as the Beatles left the stage, a girl fell from an overhead beam, landing at Ringo's feet. In Cleveland, they were physically dragged off stage while mounted police charged the arena, lassoing two hundred fans together in a giant net. . . . Each day the madness differed yet remained the same. It was cops and sweat and [thrown] jelly beans hailing in dreamlike noise; it was faces uglied by shrieking and biting fists; it was huge amphitheaters left littered with flashbulbs and hair rollers and buttons and badges and hundreds of pairs of knickers, wringing wet.[67]

CHANGING THE FACE OF ROCK

Advertising executives knew a good gimmick when they saw one, and the fads generated by Beatlemania quickly changed the face of American television. In 1965, *The Beatles* TV cartoon series began airing in the United States, with voice actors imitating the Liverpool slang of John, Paul, George, and Ringo. This was followed by *The Monkees*, a TV show about a make-believe band who imitated the antics of the Beatles in *A Hard Day's Night*. The Monkees—whose name was misspelled like the Beatles—became so popular that their music (originally written and performed by studio musicians) actually knocked Beatles songs from the number-one spot on the record charts.

In 1965, another hugely successful Beatle movie, *Help!* was released with an album of the same name. By this time, the band had changed not only the lives of their teenage fans but the face of popular music itself. In what was known as the "British Invasion," dozens of English bands had huge hits in America in the wake of the Beatles—with some not-so-subtly imitating Lennon or McCartney's song styles.

Records by bands such as the Rolling Stones, the Kinks, the Animals, Gerry and the Pacemakers, Herman's Hermits, Freddy and the Dreamers, and others quickly eclipsed American artists on record charts. Even Elvis's record sales paled next to pre-viously unknown bands such as the Dave Clark Five. Only the Beach Boys and Motown soul groups such as the Temptations, the Miracles, and the Supremes managed to fend off the British Invasion.

American bands such as the Byrds, the Rascals, and the Mamas and Papas were formed to stave off the British Invasion. These groups also used the Beatles' unique soaring harmonies and guitar and drum arrangements for inspiration. Lennon commented on the phenomenon:

The 1965 movie Help!, *released with an album of the same name, was another great success for the Beatles.*

Look, we copied nobody. . . . We've got our own style based on the music we grew up with, and it annoys me a lot to find groups getting on the wagon by copying sounds we were playing two years ago. Why can't these copyists make their own styles like we did? It happens in hairstyles as well. I see players in some groups have even the same length of hair as us. . . . The difference between the Beatles and some of these others is that we didn't sit around in the pool saying: "We're going to be big stars." Music was part of our lives. We played it because we loved doing it, not just for the loot. Unlike some groups, we don't go around even now saying: "Look, we're stars." I just consider myself a lucky layabout from Liverpool who has had some success.[68]

"THINKING ABOUT MY OWN EMOTIONS"

As Lennon adjusted to becoming an overnight sensation, he found that his boyhood home on Menlove Avenue had been turned into a shrine by adoring fans. His aunt Mimi, now living alone, was besieged daily by the press and hysterical fans. Her phone rang constantly with reporters and love-sick girls trying to find her nephew.

Mimi was finally forced to move from the home she loved. Luckily, Lennon was able to buy her a luxurious house in Poole, Dorset, a resort community. Even there it was hard to find peace—guide boats soon put the house on their sightseeing tours. Lennon never forgot his aunt, however, and continued to visit her while in town or

A hysterical fan screams at a Beatles concert. Adoring female fans often called Lennon's aunt Mimi in search of her nephew.

call her several times a week from wherever he was playing.

When he wasn't with his aunt, Lennon began to drink heavily to cope with the pressures of stardom. He now partied with American pop stars such as Fats Domino, the Righteous Brothers, and Ray Charles. But after three or four scotch-and-cokes, Lennon sometimes shocked his rock-and-roll friends with his aggressive and argumentative behavior. As Coleman writes, "This was not the cosy Beatle whose moptop image had been pumped across the Atlantic as something clean and pure. Here was a drunk!"[69]

Lennon had been drinking since he was a teenager, and had been exposed to plenty of drugs in Hamburg. But the entire tone of the Beatles' music changed when the musical sage Bob Dylan first smoked marijuana with the group while they were working on *Help!* in 1965. By this time, Dylan was a huge international star on nearly equal footing with the Beatles, having written such immortal songs as "The Times They Are A-Changin'," "Like a Rolling Stone," and "Mr. Tambourine Man."

After the meeting, Lennon entered what he called his "Dylan period." Instead of writing commercial love songs with little depth, Lennon began to put his own emotions into the songs, commenting,

> [The song] "You've Got To Hide Your Love Away" is my Dylan period. It's one of those things that you sing a bit sadly to yourself, "Here I stand head in hand . . ." I'd started thinking about my own emotions. I don't know when exactly it started . . . [the songs] "I'm A Loser" or "Hide Your Love Away," those kinds of things. Instead of projecting myself into a situation, I would try to express what I felt about myself, which I'd done in my books. I think it was Dylan who helped me realize that . . . by hearing his work.[70]

A CHANGING SOUND

After the success of *Help!* the Beatles released *Rubber Soul*. This was their sixth album in three years, recorded after their second feature film. In addition they continued to tour the world practically nonstop in the midst of Beatlemania madness. And John Lennon had only just turned twenty-five.

On *Rubber Soul*, Lennon continued to reinvent his music, forging a dynamic blend of sweet acoustic guitars, jangling electric guitars, and lilting bass lines that were unique in pop music. Harrison added to the mix by playing a traditional Indian instrument known as a sitar on Lennon's song "Norwegian Wood." This was the first time that the sitar was heard by most rock fans, but not the last. Soon dozens of other bands, including the Rolling Stones, began to use the sound of the sitar layered within their rock songs.

The hypnotic sound of the sitar provided a perfect soundtrack for the rapidly changing social scene of the mid-1960s. A relatively new drug, LSD, also called "acid," was gaining popularity among trendsetters in Britain and the United States. This drug helped spawn the hippie movement that swept across the Western world at this time. The cute "moptops" and Beatle boots of the early '60s gave way to shoulder- or waist-length hair, beards, beads, moccasins, sandals, and rainbow-colored clothing.

LSD was so powerful and so potent that it changed its users in profound ways, causing them to "lose their ego," believe they had seen God or the devil, or believe they had witnessed the creation of the universe. When John Lennon and George Harrison took the drug in late 1965, it would also help influence a new generation of musical experimentation.

"EVERYTHING WAS PERFECT"

LSD first grabbed hold of the Beatles one night when Lennon, Harrison, and their wives were dining with a dentist they had recently met in London. The dentist secretly dropped large doses of LSD into his guests' after-dinner coffees—without taking any

AWARDED BY THE QUEEN

On October 16, 1965, the Beatles were awarded Britain's highest honor—an MBE, or Member of the Order of the British Empire medal. The award was usually given to soldiers who had acted heroically in battle, and when it was announced that a long-haired group of rock musicians were to receive the medal, hundreds of soldiers returned their medals to the queen in protest. In The Beatles Anthology, *Lennon describes his comical indifference at the prestigious awards ceremony administered by the queen of England.*

"Taking the MBE was a sell-out for me. We thought being offered the MBE was . . . funny. . . . Why? What for? We all met and agreed it was daft. . . . We all said 'Let's not.' Then it all just seemed part of the game we'd agreed to play. . . . We'd nothing to lose, except that bit of you which said you didn't believe in it.

Although we don't believe in the Royal Family, you can't help being impressed when you're in the palace, when you know you're standing in front of the Queen. It was like a dream. It was beautiful. People were playing music. . . . It was historical. It was like being in a museum. . . .

To start with, we want to laugh. But when it happens to you, when you're being decorated, you don't laugh anymore. We, however, were giggling like crazy because we smoked a joint in the [bathroom] at Buckingham Palace, we were so nervous."

The Beatles pose with their MBE medals. The medals were usually awarded to soldiers who had acted heroically in battle.

himself. After dinner, the group traveled to a nightclub, where they were soon experiencing the wildest trips of their lives.

At this time, people in England knew very little about LSD, and the dentist simply thought that taking acid was like smoking strong marijuana. It was not, and as the drug began to take effect, Harrison described the evening:

> Suddenly I felt the most incredible feeling come over me. It was something like a very concentrated version of the best feeling I've ever had in my whole life. It was fantastic. *I fell in love*, not with anything or anybody in particular but with *everything*. Everything was perfect, in a perfect light, and I had an overwhelming desire to go round the club telling everybody how much I loved them—people I'd never seen before.[71]

After several hours, Harrison managed to drive everyone to his home, but as the drug was wearing off, Lennon imagined that Harrison's house was a giant submarine. This imagery would appear on the Beatles' next album in the song "Yellow Submarine."

Lennon's experience with LSD profoundly changed him. Cynthia said that "It opened the floodgates of his mind and he seemed to escape from the imprisonment of fame. Tensions, bad tempers, were replaced by understanding and love as his message."[72]

"More Popular than Jesus"

Lennon's drug use remained a secret, but it might have caused him to let his guard down when speaking to a reporter from the London *Evening Standard* during a March 1966 interview. Lennon's comments created the largest—and ugliest—Beatles controversy to date.

When Lennon spoke to the reporter, he had been intently studying Western religion. He gave his frank opinion about Christianity, saying,

> Christianity will go. It will vanish and shrink. I needn't argue with that; I'm right and I will be proven right. [The Beatles are] more popular than Jesus now; I don't know which will go first—rock 'n' roll or Christianity. Jesus was all right but his disciples were thick [stupid] and ordinary. It's them twisting it that ruins it for me.[73]

When Lennon's comment was printed in England in the middle of the long interview, it went mostly unnoticed. In fact, the article was praised by some as proof that pop stars can also be intellectuals and comment on subjects other than music. Several English ministers also supported Lennon's point, saying that they considered it to be a problem that there seemed to be more people attending Beatles concerts than church on Sunday.

Four months later, however, the comment appeared in the U.S. teen magazine *Datebook*, without the rest of the article. In fact, the comment was featured on a banner front-page headline.

Americans reacted with outrage. Two weeks before the Beatles were about to begin a huge American tour, John Lennon was at the center of a violent controversy. In the Deep South, anti-Beatles demon-

To protest Lennon's comment that the Beatles were more popular than Jesus, teenagers burn Beatles' records at a bonfire.

strations were held in dozens of cities. People burned Beatles records and paraphernalia at huge public bonfires, and thirty-five radio stations banned the band's music. Several ministers threatened to excommunicate members of their congregations who attended Beatles concerts.

Concert promoters said that they could not guarantee the band's safety on the upcoming tour. Some said, however, that if Lennon apologized, things might calm down. Lennon at first refused but relented after breaking down in tears over how his words would affect the careers of his bandmates. Meanwhile, Beatles hate mail and death threats were arriving at the Beatles' headquarters daily, some sarcastically addressed to "Jesus Lennon." Finally, at a Beatles press conference in Chicago at the beginning of the tour, an ashen-faced Lennon offered an apology.

"WE'VE HAD ENOUGH"

During the summer tour of 1966, though, the protests and death threats continued.

LENNON'S APOLOGY

When Lennon said the Beatles were more popular than Jesus, he touched off a firestorm in America that resulted in death threats and people burning Beatles records in bonfires in dozens of cities. At a press conference in Chicago, the shaken Lennon attempted to explain his remarks, excerpted here from The Beatles Anthology.

"If I'd have said, 'Television is more popular than Jesus,' I might have got away with it. I am sorry I opened my mouth. . . . I said [the Beatles] are having more influence on kids and things than anything else, including Jesus. I said it in that way, which was the wrong way. I'm not anti-God, anti-Christ, or antireligion. I was not knocking it. I was not saying we are greater or better. I think it's a bit silly. . . .

When I first heard about the repercussions I thought, 'It can't be true'. . . . And then when I realised it was serious, I was worried stiff because I knew how it would go on, and the things that would get said about it, and all those miserable pictures of me looking like a cynic, and it would go on and on and on and get out of hand, and I couldn't control it. I can't answer for it when it gets that big, because it's nothing to do with me then.

I'm sorry I said it for the mess it's made, but I never meant it as an antireligious thing. My views are from what I've read or observed of Christianity, and what it was, and what it has been, and what it could be. I'm not knocking it or saying it's bad. I'm just saying it seems to be shrinking and losing context. Nothing seems to be replacing it."

At a Memphis concert, where the Ku Klux Klan was burning Beatles records outside, someone set off a firecracker. Lennon said, "Every one of us looked at each other, because each thought it was the other that had been shot. It was that bad."[74]

Besides the hatred generated by Lennon's "Jesus" remark, the insanity of touring was wearing down the band. In Manila in the Philippines, band members were kicked and punched by soldiers for turning down a party invitation from Imelda Marcos, the president's wife. Upon leaving the country, Epstein was forced to return all the money the band had made at the concert they had played. In other foreign locations, the band faced protests, riots, hurricanes, and other life-threatening events.

John, Paul, George, and Ringo unanimously agreed that the music was suffering and that they preferred the safe confines of the recording studio to the pandemonium of live shows. In August 1966, the Beatles played Candlestick Park in San Francisco. Although they did not know it at the time, after more than fourteen hundred live shows, this was to be the last concert performance for the world's most famous band.

As Lennon later said, "We've had enough of performing forever. I can't imagine any reason which would make us do any sort of tour again. We're all really tired. It does nothing for us anymore."[75]

5 Idealism, Energy, Music and Money

When the Beatles announced that they would stop touring and only make records, their fans were stunned. No popular group had ever voluntarily walked away from the lucrative concert business. But Lennon said that the Beatles were more than performers—they were artists like poets, painters, and authors. And besides, the world had changed drastically in the few years since "I Want to Hold Your Hand" had been recorded.

By 1966, the United States and Western Europe were chaotic as the Vietnam War raged in Southeast Asia and hundreds of thousands of young people protested the conflict. Meanwhile, millions of people were taking drugs such as marijuana and LSD, dropping out of society, and experimenting with "free love." While John Lennon and the Beatles had a profound effect on music and fashion in earlier years, the influence of LSD could now be heard on Lennon's songs, which were quickly becoming the soundtrack for the counterculture.

LAYERING SOUNDS

The Beatles began recording their next album, *Revolver*, after Lennon's first LSD ex-perience, and the results were obvious. At this point, Starr and McCartney had not yet taken the drug, and *Revolver* clearly shows the split within the band. Lennon's acid-drenched vocals fill out such expansive songs as "I'm Only Sleeping," "Tomorrow Never Knows," and "She Said She Said." Meanwhile, McCartney is at his "moptop" best with sensitive love songs such as "Here, There, and Everywhere" and "Good Day Sunshine," plus whimsical numbers complete with sound effects such as "Yellow Submarine." This marked difference in tone showed the Beatles' celebrated song-writing team moving in distinctly separate directions.

Once again, Lennon's songs had a pervasive influence on many who heard them. The lyrics for "Tomorrow Never Knows," for instance, were based on the *Tibetan Book of the Dead*, an ancient text that holy men read to dying Tibetans to help them on their journey through death and rebirth. No one had ever drawn on such heavy existential concepts for a rock song before.

At this time, Lennon and the others were also inspired to take control of production, working with George Martin to add a new array of bizarre sound effects and instrumentation to the music. Although they still recorded on four-track tape equipment that would be extremely primitive by today's standards, Lennon and the others filled in songs with backward guitar licks, distortion, filters, and unconventional musical instruments. The Beatles added violins, cellos, trumpets, French horns, and other instruments traditionally associated with classical music. To get the bubbly sounds on "Yellow Submarine," Lennon blew through a straw in a glass of water.

To elicit as many sounds as possible, Lennon piled sound over sound on the same small piece of recording tape. The richness of these "tape loops" would later

be imitated in the '70s by transistorized "effects pedals," and in the '80s by digital computers, but in 1966, it was up to the Beatles to "invent" dozens of new sounds and present them to a waiting world. In *The Beatles Recording Sessions*, Mark Lewisohn describes how these studio techniques worked in "Tomorrow Never Knows," the first song Lennon recorded after taking LSD:

> "Tomorrow Never Knows" . . . was a heavy metal recording of enormous proportions, with thundering echo and booming, quivering, ocean-bed vibrations. And peeking out from under the

Protesters of the Vietnam War run through Central Park. Lennon's songs became the soundtrack of the antiwar movement.

squall was John Lennon's voice, supremely eerie, as if it were being broadcast through the cheapest transistor radio . . . and delivering the most bizarre Beatles lyric yet.[76]

"STRAWBERRY FIELDS FOREVER"

By late 1966, the Beatles had stopped touring, and rumors of a Beatle breakup constantly circulated in the press. With little comment about the gossip, the band went back into the recording studio to work on a new project. Up until this time, the Beatles had been producing two 14-song LPs a year for three years. But McCartney and Starr had also taken LSD several times by now, and Lennon was taking it all the time. The Beatles were not in the mood to crank out another album full of three-minute pop songs.

The first song they recorded, "Strawberry Fields Forever," was written by Lennon while he was making a movie in Spain. The whimsical and dreamlike song contrasts the unreality of the drug experience with childhood memories. The title was taken from the Salvation Army Children's Home, an orphanage named Strawberry Fields, near Lennon's boyhood home.

Producer George Martin framed "Strawberry Fields Forever" with tape loops and an extremely primitive electric synthesizer called a Mellotron, and added a swirling "sound picture" marked by Starr's drum cymbals played backwards. Martin, the band, and studio musicians also supplemented the sound with trumpets, cellos,

and a harplike Indian instrument called a swordmandel played by Harrison.

In *With a Little Help from My Friends: The Making of Sgt. Pepper*, Martin gives his opinion of the musical masterpiece:

> Way ahead of its time, strong, complicated both in concept and execution, highly original and quickly labelled "psychedelic", "Strawberry Fields Forever" was the work of an undoubted genius. We could not have produced a better prototype for the future. The care and attention we lavished on that track, its technical and musical excellence . . . we were all very proud of our new baby. For my money, it was the most original and inventive track to date in pop music.[77]

"Strawberry Fields Forever" was released as a single in March 1967, where it went to number one, backed by "Penny Lane," a McCartney song about his childhood. A short music video of the song (one of the first ever made) was also filmed. The video was a surrealistic vision of the Beatles playing in a large tree, with the film running backwards. The band once again changed fashion standards when they appeared with handlebar mustaches and "shag" haircuts, which were not commonly seen at the time.

SGT. PEPPER'S LONELY HEARTS CLUB BAND

When "Strawberry Fields Forever" was released, the Beatles were already busy recording their next album, *Sgt. Pepper's Lonely Hearts Club Band*. Unlike the business

How I Won the War

When the Beatles stopped touring in the autumn of 1966, John Lennon did not go home. Instead he went to Spain to take his first (and last) serious acting role in the film *How I Won the War* directed by Richard Lester, who had directed *A Hard Day's Night*. By this time, the United States, with Great Britain's support, was deeply involved in the Vietnam War, and Lennon was an early opponent of the conflict. In the film, Lennon plays a World War II soldier who opposes all war.

For his role in the movie, Lennon cut his hair short and wore round wire-framed spectacles. Although he had refused to wear such glasses when he was younger, Lennon continued to wear them after the film was over. Once again, John Lennon inadvertently began another fad. Thousands of people started to wear what Americans called "granny glasses" exactly like Lennon's.

After the film wrapped up, Lennon joined the Campaign for Nuclear Disarmament and privately spoke out about the Vietnam War. At Epstein's urging, however, the musician kept his thoughts to himself. The Beatles' manager was adamant about deflecting any political controversy away from the lovable "moptops."

Lennon played the role of a soldier in How I Won the War. *His glasses started another fad in America.*

hours they kept in earlier years, the band was now entering the studio at 8:00 P.M. and working until dawn.

Although Lennon did not use drugs in the studio, he continued to take LSD with alarming regularity at home. His wife, Cynthia, however, had bad experiences with the drug and refused to partake in anymore acid trips. Coupled with the hours spent away from home, Lennon's

The Beatles experimented with new sounds for Sgt. Pepper's Lonely Hearts Club Band. *The revolutionary album was an instant success.*

drug use was driving a wedge into his marriage.

From December 6, 1966, until April 20, 1967, the Beatles were submerged in the recording process. Hour after hour was spent attempting to create previously unheard-of sounds. Lennon even asked to be suspended from the studio ceiling above a microphone by a rope tied around his waist. He wanted to get a "phase shifting" sound by singing while twirling dizzily in a rapid circle. Although this never happened, Lennon and Martin incorporated many other sounds, including the forty-one members of the London Symphony Orchestra playing a cacophonous free-form finale to "A Day in the Life."

When *Sgt. Pepper's* was released on June 1, 1967, the Beatles were nervous. They weren't sure if the pop-record-buying public was ready for such a musically advanced album. When the album sold 250,000 in its first week of release, and 2.5 million copies by August, however, Lennon knew that the world was ready for a new level of musical experimentation.

In 1967, *Sgt. Pepper's* instantly became the soundtrack for what became known as the Summer of Love. As Martin writes, "[*Sgt. Pepper's* succeeded] in speaking for its age, capturing the sixties and much of what that era came to stand for in sound: the psychedelia, the fashions, the vogue for Eastern mysticism, the spirit of adventure, the whole peace and love thing, the anti-war movement; it was all there and more."[78]

Sgt. Pepper's was the first rock "concept" album, meaning the music was continuous and had no pauses between songs. The album cover alone was enough to thrill some people. The photo showed the Beatles as if they had been transformed into another group altogether—Sgt. Pepper's Lonely Hearts Club Band. They were surrounded by cardboard cutouts of famous—and infamous—people such as actress Mae West and the late comedian Lenny Bruce. It was also one of the first albums to open to double size, and the first to have song lyrics printed inside.

Fueled by LSD and other mind-altering substances, fans studied every word written

THE SUMMER OF LOVE

The Beatles released Sgt. Pepper's Lonely Hearts Club Band *in June 1967, at the beginning of the hippie phenomenon known as the Summer of Love. In the book* With a Little Help from My Friends: The Making of Sgt. Pepper, *Beatles producer George Martin describes his feelings about those times.*

"It was the Summer of Love.

US Air Force B-52s were dropping 800 tons of bombs a day on North Vietnam; [Chinese leader] Mao Zedong's Red Guards had the whole of China by the throat; and . . . people were starving [in the African nation of Biafra] when they were not being massacred.

But from where I was sitting, [recording the Beatles] at EMI's Abbey Road studios in west London, people in the thousands were giving themselves over to Peace and Love. They were dropping out, growing their hair, painting their bodies, and inventing [free love]. They contemplated revolution, and their navels. Flowers gave them power. They had pot and acid, optimism and enthusiasm. They had "happenings", "be-ins" and "love-ins". They had idealism, energy, money and youth. And they had one other thing. They had music. The good vibrations kept on coming, from [Jimi] Hendrix and the Who, from [Mick] Jagger and from [Janis] Joplin, from [Bob] Dylan and the Beach Boys and the Doors and . . . [soul music from] Motown. In flats . . . peacecamps and parks, in huts and highrises and apartments the world over: they were listening. From Rio to Rimini, Dallas to Djibouti—in their millions they turned on and tuned in.

On 1 June 1967 they heard the clarion call, the toppermost, poppermost sound of an entire generation. It was a groundbreaking album by the Beatles. It was Hippy Symphony No. 1. It was called *Sgt. Pepper's Lonely Hearts Club Band.*

And it was, after all, the Summer of Love."

The Summer of Love in 1967 was a time of experimentation in drugs, love, and music.

on the rainbow-colored album looking for hidden messages. Some played the songs backward searching for the Beatles' answer to life. "A Day in the Life" was even supposed to reveal an obscene sentence when played backward. Norman comments on this phenomenon and Lennon's reaction to it:

> Of all the properties imagined in *Sergeant Pepper*, the most pervasive was that of actual magic. It was believed to hold prophecies, messages and signs. It marked the beginning of a search, among Beatles music . . . for further prophecies, messages and signs. . . . [The] Beatles . . . hated the mystery and message-seekers. . . . John, especially, denied with increasing bitterness that his songs had any motive whatever. "I just shove a lot of sounds together, then shove some words on. . . . We know we're conning people, because people want to be conned. They give us the freedom to con them." [79]

While the fans attempted to decipher the lyrics, praise for *Sgt. Pepper's* came from all corners. Kenneth Tynan, a reporter for the prestigious *London Times*, called the album "a decisive moment in the history of Western civilization," and the *New York Times Review of Books* said the album was "a new and golden Renaissance of Song." [80] Dr. Timothy Leary, a former psychologist who by this time was an outspoken promoter of LSD, said the Beatles were "prototypes of evolutionary agents sent by God with the mysterious power to create a new species—a young race of laughing freemen. . . . They are the wisest, holiest, most effective avatars [God incarnations] the human race has ever produced." [81]

Not everyone was so enthralled with the album, however. The BBC, for one, banned "A Day in the Life" because the lyric "I'd love to turn you on" was believed to be a reference to drug use.

"LOVE IS THE FORCE OF LIFE"

The success of *Sgt. Pepper's* cemented the Beatles' reputation as the uncontested leaders of the love generation. They were considered legends by their fans and respected as artists by the establishment. They had more money and more fame than any rock band in history, and even as they rested, flush with success, dozens of other bands were trying to create their own versions of *Sgt. Pepper's*. But John Lennon was searching for something more.

Around this time, Harrison's wife, Pattie, introduced George to Hindu mysticism as taught by the Maharishi Mahesh Yogi. The Maharishi practiced a mental relaxation technique called transcendental meditation, and his message sounded like lyrics to a Beatles song: "Love is the sweet expression of life. It is the supreme content of life. Love is the force of life, powerful and sublime. The flower of life blooms in love and radiates love all around." [82]

Taking the guru's message to heart, the Beatles traveled to a spiritual retreat in Bangor, Wales, to learn meditation from the Maharishi. Meditation involves clearing the mind of day-to-day thoughts by chanting a short phrase, called a mantra, over and over again. By practicing this technique only

THE FIRST GLOBAL BROADCAST

When the first-ever worldwide satellite TV show was broadcast, it featured the Beatles singing "All You Need Is Love," John Lennon's message of peace and love written specifically for the show. Fred Bronson gives a behind-the-scenes description of the song and the broadcast in The Billboard Book of Number One Hits.

"[An] estimated audience of 400 million people watched the Beatles record 'All You Need Is Love' in cavernous Studio One at Abbey Road studios. . . . The recording was telecast live via satellite to 26 nations around the world on a unique six-hour television program, 'Our World'. . . . The Beatles had been selected by the BBC to be Britain's participants in the program. 'All You Need Is Love' was written [by John Lennon] in May [1967]. . . .

The Beatles invited many of their friends to the studio to form a chorus for backing vocals. Mick Jagger, Keith Richards, Brian Jones [from the Rolling Stones], Keith Moon [from the Who], Donovan, Graham Nash, Jane Asher [Paul's girlfriend], Marianne Faithfull, [and] Patti Harrison . . . were all in attendance.

Producer Martin suggested they begin the song with the *Marseillaise*, the French national anthem. It was also Martin's idea to include a fragment of Glenn Miller's 'In the Mood'. . . . The Beatles included 'Greensleeves' and a piece of their own 'She Loves You'. The six-minute version seen on the 'Our World' telecast was not released as a single. After the program, John recorded his vocal track again for a final take. It was then edited down to four minutes and released around the world. In America, 'All You Need Is Love' entered the Hot 100 at number 71 on July 22, 1967. Four weeks later it became the Beatles' 14th number one single."

The Beatles display signs of their song title "All You Need Is Love" written in different languages. The band recorded the song live on a telecast seen in twenty-six nations.

twenty minutes a day, people can achieve extreme relaxation, creative inspiration, and mental clarity.

At this time, few people in the United States had heard of yoga or meditation. Like almost everything else that the Beatles tried, though, the fad of Indian mysticism quickly swept through the Western world.

Although this turn to Indian spirituality shocked some Beatles fans, it did wonders for the band. They all stopped taking drugs, as Lennon explained: "If we'd met Maharishi before we had taken LSD, we wouldn't have needed to take it. . . . We don't regret having taken LSD. It was a stepping-stone. But now we should be able to experience things as first hand, instead of artificially with a wrong stepping-stone like drugs."[83]

MAGICAL MYSTERY TRIPS

On August 27, 1967, the Beatles were achieving much-deserved mental peace and relaxation in Bangor. But reality intruded on their sheltered world once again when they received news that thirty-three-year-old Brian Epstein had died in London from an accidental overdose of prescription sleeping pills. Lennon was especially close to the Beatles' manager, and once again he lost a best friend and confidant. Lennon was comforted, however, by his newfound Indian philosophies, stating, "Brian has died only in body, and his spirit will always be working with us. His power and force were everything, and his power and his force will linger on."[84]

With Epstein gone, the Beatles were adrift with no manager. Although Epstein had played a smaller role after the band stopped touring, the Beatles sat atop a marketing empire worth hundreds of millions of dollars. And though the Beatles were brilliant musicians and songwriters, they had little experience in business.

McCartney however, appointed himself to take on Epstein's former role. The bass player's first project—a sixty-minute television program—proved to be disastrous. The show, titled the *Magical Mystery Tour*, followed the Beatles as they drove around the English countryside in a psychedelically painted bus with a group of circus performers and other weird characters. When it was shown in England on December 26, 1967, only about 15 million people watched it. Although many Beatles fans loved the special, London critics mercilessly slammed it, calling the show "chaotic," "appalling," "a colossal conceit," and "blatant rubbish."[85] As a result of these terrible reviews, the million-dollar deal for U.S. broadcast rights was canceled.

The Beatles were comforted, however, when the *Magical Mystery Tour* album sold more than 2 million copies in December 1967 alone. Once again, Lennon contributed several lush recordings (he called them "sound paintings") to the album, including "I Am the Walrus," a song very loosely based on the poem "The Walrus and the Carpenter" from *Alice in Wonderland*.

MEDITATING WITH THE MAHARISHI

Although the album was selling well, the failed *Magical Mystery Tour* TV special upset the band. Thus, feeling they were in need of further spiritual enlightenment, the

Lennon and the Beatles followed the teachings of the Maharishi (far right) for almost a year but became disillusioned after the guru allegedly harassed an actress at an Indian retreat.

Beatles, their wives, and a small group of movie and rock stars journeyed to India in early 1968 to visit the Maharishi's meditation academy in Rishikesh at the foot of the Himalayas. During his eight-week stay at the academy, Lennon meditated up to eight hours a day. Away from drugs and alcohol, and inspired by the sharpest mental clarity he had experienced in years, he also wrote dozens of songs.

After several weeks at the retreat, there was a rumor (which remains unsubstantiated) that the Maharishi had sexually harassed actress Mia Farrow, who had accompanied the Beatles there. Lennon be-

lieved that the story was true and confronted the guru. When the Maharishi asked Lennon why he was leaving, the musician answered bitterly, "If you're so bloody cosmic, you'll know why."[86]

Although Lennon may have been disappointed in the guru's alleged behavior, he continued to practice meditation. Having been looked on as a guru himself, Lennon clearly understood the folly of placing one's beliefs in another person.

While in India, unbeknownst to Cynthia, Lennon had been writing long letters to Yoko Ono, a Japanese conceptual artist in London. Lennon had met Ono at her art opening in November 1966. At the time, Lennon was fascinated with Ono's absurd abstract concepts of art, and the two were instantly attracted to each other.

When Lennon returned to London in March 1968, he invited Ono to his mansion while his wife was on vacation in Greece. Lennon and Ono spent the evening experimenting with electronic music and abstract noise. The next morning Cynthia returned home to find John and Yoko making tea in the kitchen. Cynthia was shattered when she realized Yoko was wearing one of her kimonos. Lennon soon announced to his wife that he was in love with Ono, and within months Cynthia and John were divorced. And once again, Lennon resumed his steady diet of pot, acid, and alcohol.

WHEN JOHN MET YOKO

John Lennon met his future wife Yoko Ono at Ono's art exhibit in London in 1966. The event is described by Jerry Hopkins in Yoko Ono.

"Lennon [wandered] around the gallery. The Beatle stopped at a pedestal and picked up something labeled 'Box of Smile.' He opened the lid and saw his face reflected in a mirror. He smiled.

A few minutes later, John stopped beside a white ladder. On the ceiling above was a black canvas with a tiny white dot in the center. Hanging from the painting was a magnifying glass on a chain. 'I climbed the ladder, looked through the spy glass, and in tiny letters it said, "Yes,"' John [said.] 'So it was positive. I felt relieved. I was very impressed.'

John remembered that Yoko met him at the bottom of the ladder, where she handed him a card. It said 'Breathe' on it. John stuck out his tongue and began to pant heavily. 'Like that?' he asked.

[Gallery owner John] Dunbar approached and introduced them. Yoko apparently made no sign that she recognized John's face or name.

John turned to a nearby canvas and saw a jar of nails and a hammer. A sign read, 'Hammer a Nail In.'

'D'ya mind if I have a go?' he asked. 'Hammer a nail?'...

She answered in her small, lilting voice, 'It will cost you two shillings.'

John smiled and said, 'I'll give you an imaginary two shillings and hammer an imaginary nail.'

On his way out of the gallery, John picked up an apple from another pedestal, and after smiling at the £200 [$500] price tag, he took a bite and replaced the apple on the pedestal."

Apple Corps

The upheavals in Lennon's personal life were matched by turmoil in his professional one. Without Epstein's guiding hand, the Beatles had set up their own corporation, dubbed Apple Corps (pronounced "core") by McCartney. The company was divided into several subsidiaries such as Apple Retail, Apple Music, Apple Films, and Apple Records. The band brought in some of their old friends, often at excessive salaries, to run the different departments. On April 15, the Beatles announced the business launch to the American press.

Apple bought a four-story building in the heart of London's largest shopping district, covered it with a huge psychedelic painting, and opened a boutique. Lennon refused to hire professionals to run it; instead, he hired his childhood friend Pete Shotton to manage the store. And Shotton later said that Lennon "persisted in staffing the boutique with hippies whose sole qualification was that they liked to smoke dope as much as the Beatles did." [87]

The daily business decisions at Apple Corps had to be approved by a resident psychic who used Tarot cards, the *I Ching,* and astrology to peer into the future. Meanwhile, the business executives in the company spent their days eating in fancy restaurants, drinking expensive liquor, and traveling on the Beatles' expense account. For the weekly business meetings, Lennon would arrive high on LSD, while Starr stretched out on the couch to take a nap. The Beatles soon bought another building on the prestigious Savile Row to use as a recording studio and offices for Apple Records.

The London headquarters for Apple Corps, the Beatles corporation, included a boutique staffed by pot-smoking hippies.

Apple personnel engaged in many failed, drug-induced schemes, but they found success with the kaleidoscopic cartoon "Yellow Submarine," released in the spring of 1968. The innovative story, about the Beatles traveling through a psychedelic world in a yellow submarine and saving the world from the "Blue Meanies" with music, was an instant classic.

"You Say You Want a Revolution"

When the Beatles returned to the recording studio in 1968, Lennon, McCartney, and

Harrison had all built up a backlog of songs while meditating in India. Even Starr had written a tune for the first time. Pandemonium, however, swirled around the Beatles.

The recording division of Apple Corps was financially sound, but other experimental businesses were losing massive amounts of money. The offices of Apple were constantly filled with unsavory drug dealers, stoned hippies, half-clothed groupies, and even members of the Hell's Angels motorcycle gang. Some people were actually stealing telephones, files, typewriters, and artwork off the walls.

The rest of the world had exploded into chaos as well. The peaceful anti-Vietnam War protests of earlier years had turned violent and bloody. The United States was rocked by the assassination of civil rights leader Martin Luther King Jr., which led to massive riots in hundreds of African American neighborhoods across the country. Months later, antiwar presidential candidate Robert Kennedy was also murdered. Black and white political radicals alike were preaching the violent overthrow of the U.S. government.

In the midst of this youth rebellion, Lennon added fuel to the fire by releasing the single "Revolution," with McCartney's "Hey Jude" on the other side. "Hey Jude" was written for Lennon's son Julian, who was shattered by his parents' divorce, but it was "Revolution" that caused the controversy.

The Beatles had been using their sophisticated marketing strategy to sell love and peace for several years. But militant revolutionaries were eager to harness the power that the rock stars had over young people. "Revolution" at first listen seemed to sup-port fierce political rebellion. It was certainly read that way by both politicians and radicals. As had happened before, however, people seriously misread Lennon's lyrics. In the song, the singer says he wants no part in violence or destruction, later telling *Playboy* magazine,

> The statement in "Revolution" was mine. The lyrics stand today. They're still my feeling about politics: I want to see the *plan*. That is what I used to say to [revolutionary leaders] Jerry Rubin and Abbie Hoffman. Count me out if it's for violence. Don't expect me on the [police] barricades unless it is with flowers. As far as overthrowing something in the name of Marxism or Christianity, I want to know what you're going to do *after* you've knocked it all down. I mean, can't we use *some* of it? What's the point of bombing Wall Street? If you want to change the system, change the system. It's no good shooting people.[88]

DISAGREEMENT WITHIN THE BAND

Meanwhile, another sort of revolution was taking place within the closed circle of the Beatles as they recorded their next album. Yoko Ono and John Lennon had become inseparable, and Ono now sat by Lennon's side all day in the recording studio. According to *Yoko Ono* by Jerry Hopkins, "this violated a long-standing agreement [the Beatles] had about never bringing wives or girlfriends to recording sessions . . . [and there] is no argument about the reaction to Yoko's presence. The other Beatles didn't like it."[89]

For her part, Ono was extremely intimidated by the scene, and so she sat quietly, usually speaking only to Lennon by whispering in his ear. The other band members, though, interpreted Ono's behavior as snobbish. When she ventured to make a few critical comments about the other Beatles' work, the band was aghast. Only George Martin was allowed that privilege. To Ono, the clashing of the egos seemed ridiculous, as she later told *Playboy* magazine: "I met an interesting guy and we got together, and suddenly he's got these three [disapproving] in-laws . . . meaning Paul, George, and Ringo." [90]

BITTER BACKLASH

When Lennon's love affair with Ono was discovered by the press, it brought forth public outrage from Beatles critics and fans alike. During an Ono art exhibition sponsored by Lennon, he told the assembled press, "I'm in love with her." [91] Within days, they were receiving letters from Beatles "fans" filled with hateful language, racial insults, and even death threats. At the time, it was considered extremely controversial for a Caucasian person, especially one of Lennon's wealth and fame, to date an Asian. In addition, Ono, who was seven

The love affair between Lennon and Yoko Ono caused an uproar among the general public and within the band. Fans objected to the interracial union and the band was angry because Lennon brought Yoko to recording sessions.

years older than Lennon, was seen as a "homewrecker" for breaking up Lennon's marriage. And she herself was married and had a five-year-old daughter.

Back in the studio to record *The White Album*, the Beatles' first two-record album, the band fragmented into three separate entities. Lennon would record his songs playing as many of the back-up instruments as possible, using Starr on the drums. Harrison brought in musicians such as Eric Clapton to work on his material. And McCartney recorded songs on which he played most of the instruments including drums, much to Starr's chagrin.

The joyous circuslike atmosphere of the *Sgt. Pepper's* days seemed to have occurred in another era. And Lennon could see the end of the Beatles in sight, later commenting, "The Beatles [really] broke up after Brian died. We made the double album, the set . . . [but] it's like if you took each track off . . . it was just me and a backing group, Paul and a backing group . . . and I enjoyed it, but we broke up then."[92]

Unlike *Sgt. Pepper's* with its smooth transitions from song to song, *The White Album* proved to be as chaotic as the times. Song styles ran the gamut from the doo-wop surf sound of "Back in the U.S.S.R." to Lennon's proto-punk "Everybody's Got Something to Hide Except for Me and My Monkey." At just over eight minutes, Lennon's "Revolution 9" was a sound-effects montage recorded with Ono consisting of thirty tape loops layered one on top of the other. Lennon was fascinated with the experimental music, telling everyone who would listen, "*This* is the music of the future. . . . You can forget [everything else] we've done—this is *it!*"[93]

"We're All Naked, Really"

By the time Lennon was putting the finishing touches on *The White Album*, Yoko Ono was pregnant, and the couple had moved into a London apartment owned by Ringo Starr. To celebrate their union, Lennon and Ono decided to release *Unfinished Music No. 1: Two Virgins*, the long tape of experimental sound effects they had made on their first date. The front cover of the album showed a picture of Lennon and Ono holding hands and standing together stark naked. The back cover showed them from behind. Lennon innocently explained, "It just seemed natural for us. . . . We're all naked, really."[94]

Although Lennon may have thought the idea a good one, in 1968 pictures of full frontal nudity were considered illegal pornography in the United States and elsewhere. EMI, the company that distributed Beatles records, refused to have anything to do with *Two Virgins*, and magazines would not accept advertisements for the album. When *Two Virgins* was finally released in January 1969, thirty thousand copies were confiscated in New Jersey because of its "pornographic" cover. Those close to the Beatles thought Lennon had lost his mind. After carefully crafting their sound and image for so many years, the sight of the less-than-physically-fit naked couple on an album cover was embarrassing.

Meanwhile, Lennon's flamboyant behavior drew the attention of a London detective named Norman Pilcher who had recently arrested members of the Rolling Stones on drug charges. On October 18, 1968, six policemen, one policewoman, and two drug-sniffing dogs invaded Lennon's London flat, finding a minuscule amount of hashish.

Lennon had been warned by a reporter the day before that the police were coming and had scoured the apartment for drugs. It was obvious to Lennon that the drugs had been planted by the police. Nevertheless, the London tabloid press snapped hundreds of photos as Lennon and Ono were led off to prison.

When the couple was released several hours later, the pregnant Ono suddenly doubled over in pain. She was taken to the hospital, where she would spend the next month in bed with Lennon by her side before finally having a miscarriage. Before the fetus died, however, Lennon recorded its hushed heartbeat, which he later used on a record.

A week after Ono's miscarriage, the couple pled guilty to a charge of possession and were fined around $600 apiece. Although this was a minor fine for a minor offense, the experience would haunt the couple for many years.

LET IT BE

By the beginning of 1969, McCartney feared that the Beatles were falling apart. In an attempt to reunite the band, the bass player decided to make *Let It Be*, a movie of the Beatles working together in the studio as they had done in the early days, recording basic catchy rock-and-roll songs. McCartney's efforts proved futile, however. As the filming progressed, it was obvious that the Beatles were tired of each other and that a great gulf had grown between them. Few smiles were exchanged, and while the camera focused mostly on McCartney, Lennon and Ono kept pretty much to themselves.

At the end of the movie, spirits brightened when the Beatles performed several songs on the roof of the Apple studios before the police shut them down. This finale to the movie would be imitated in countless music videos in later years.

The band's mood in *Let It Be* was so dour that the album and the movie were shelved. For all intents and purposes, the Beatles had ceased to exist, although none of them would dare to admit it.

6 John and Yoko

By the late 1960s, the Beatles were four grown men who had spent much of their youth in the glare of celebrity spotlight. While millions of young people spent the decade smoking pot and practicing free love, the Beatles had been working nearly nonstop to provide the counterculture with its mind-blowing soundtrack. And although the magic of the Beatles' music continued to astound their fans, the thrill was slipping away for the Fab Four.

By this time, the music revolution started by the Beatles was being expanded by a slew of talented musicians who were carrying on where *Sgt. Pepper's* left off. Jimi Hendrix, the Doors, the Grateful Dead, the Jefferson Airplane, and others were filling the airwaves with their own unique brand of "acid rock." As elder statesmen of the counterculture, the Beatles had drifted off to solo projects, marriage, and family. But John Lennon continued to be motivated by the message of peace, and he was determined to use his fame to make the world a better place.

A COMMERCIAL FOR PEACE

John Lennon and Yoko Ono were married on March 20, 1969, in Gibraltar, a British ter-

ritory along the coast of southeastern Spain. Since the couple knew they were going to be hounded incessantly by the press, they decided to use their fame as "a commercial for peace,"[95] as Lennon put it.

For seven days Lennon and Ono stayed in bed at the Amsterdam Hilton holding, what they called, a "bed-in" for peace. Reporters stormed the building expecting to find the couple engaged in lewd acts. Instead they found Lennon and Ono dressed in white, surrounded by flowers, and talking of peace and love. When asked why they chose to spend their honeymoon this way, Lennon answered,

> We thought "The other side has war on every day, not only on the news but on old John Wayne movies and every damn movie you see: war, war, war, war, kill, kill, kill, kill." We said, "Let's get some peace, peace, peace, peace on the headlines, just for a change!"[96]

For the next week the couple gave interviews eight hours a day and met with people from all over the world. When the event was over, Lennon officially changed his name to John Ono Lennon. Several weeks later he bought Tittenhurst Park, a huge mansion on seventy-four acres, where he moved with his new wife.

"GIVE PEACE A CHANCE"

The Lennons wanted to continue their peace campaign in the United States but were refused a visa in May 1969 because of their November 1968 drug bust. Instead the couple went to Toronto and held a bed-in at the Queen Elizabeth Hotel. There they met with rock stars, comedians, hippie spokesmen, and world leaders such as Canadian prime minister Pierre Trudeau.

On June 1 they recorded "Give Peace a Chance" from their bed, accompanied by Timothy Leary, Dickie Smothers from the Smothers Brothers comedy team, and others. When the song was released several weeks later, under the name "Plastic Ono Band," it became an instant anthem for the peace movement.

COME TOGETHER—BREAK UP

While the press and fans wondered if the formation of the Plastic Ono Band meant an end to the Beatles, John, Paul, George, and Ringo returned to the studios once again to record *Abbey Road*, named after the EMI

After getting married in Gibraltar, John and Yoko stayed in bed at the Amsterdam Hilton for a week and gave interviews to promote peace and love.

studios where they had recorded almost all of their previous albums. As he had done on *Let It Be*, McCartney dominated the sessions, with Lennon contributing only four songs, including "Come Together" and the otherworldly "Because."

Once again, Yoko Ono was by Lennon's side during the entire recording process. When she became sick one day, a bed was brought into the studios so that she could continue to be by her husband's side. Needless to say, the other band members were not happy with this development. When the band finally played together on Lennon's tribute to Ono, "I Want You (She's So Heavy)," on August 20, 1969, it was the last time all four Beatles would record together in studio.

On September 13, the Plastic Ono Band played Toronto's Rock 'n' Roll Revival concert. The band consisted of Lennon on lead vocals and rhythm guitar, Ono on keyboards and vocals, Eric Clapton on guitar, Claus Voorman (a friend from the Hamburg days) on bass, and Alan White on drums. The group had been assembled on one day's notice, and they rehearsed on the airplane on the way to the concert. Lennon hadn't played with anyone else in years and was so nervous that he vomited repeatedly before taking the stage.

The group played several rock classics such as "Blue Suede Shoes" and a new tune, "Cold Turkey," which Lennon had written about kicking heroin (it seemed that Ono and Lennon had been using the drug for several months but were now off it). The Plastic Ono Band also played two long Ono compositions. Yoko's shrieking, caterwauling vocals, however, did not endear her to the gathered fans, although her style would inspire female punk rock singers after the songs appeared on the album *The Plastic Ono Band—Live Peace in Toronto 1969*.

In October, Lennon returned his MBE (Member of the Order of the British Empire medal) to the queen in protest of England's support of the Vietnam War, among other things. This action created more controversy than his having accepted the medal in the first place.

LENNON CALLS IT QUITS

On September 20, 1969, unbeknownst to anyone but the other band members, John Lennon quit the Beatles. At the urging of McCartney and the Beatles' management, however, he kept this bombshell a secret from the press. The Beatles had conquered the world, changed how people looked, talked, acted, played, and listened to music. Now it was over. And John Lennon was not yet twenty-nine years old.

Several months after Lennon decided to leave the group, *Abbey Road* was released. Hailed by fans and critics as a masterpiece, the album shot to the top of the charts. Meanwhile, the rough-edged *Let It Be* album, and the accompanying movie, sat on the shelves at Apple Records. With hundreds of thousands of dollars tied up in the project, the album was finally released in March 1970, with almost 4 million advance orders for the record.

Then, on April 10, 1970, Paul McCartney gave a press conference announcing the release of his first solo album, *McCartney*. The Beatles' bass player also announced that he

"WAR IS OVER IF YOU WANT IT"

In 1969, John Lennon and Yoko Ono wanted to inspire people to imagine that the Vietnam War was over even though it continued at an extremely bloody pace. As part of their ongoing peace campaign, the Lennons invested a considerable amount of money to place billboards that said this in cities across the globe. Jon Wiener explains in Come Together: John Lennon in His Own Time:

"In December John and Yoko launched their 'War Is Over' campaign, buying billboard space in London, New York, Hollywood, Toronto, Paris, Rome, Berlin, Athens, and Tokyo. The billboards read, 'War Is Over—If You Want It—Happy Christmas, John and Yoko.' To open the campaign, John and Yoko played a 'War Is Over' benefit concert for UNICEF at the Lyceum Theatre in London, John's first live concert in England in four years. George Harrison, Eric Clapton, Billy Preston, and Keith Moon joined him onstage, probably the greatest Plastic Ono Band ever assembled. They played a screaming fifteen-minute version of 'Cold Turkey.' [The magazine] *Rolling Stone* wrote that John 'showed the crowd that his fervor for peace and Yoko hadn't dimmed his talent or displaced his sense of humor. . . . The locals still loved him.'. . .

Not everyone understood John and Yoko's 'War Is Over' campaign . . . [but Lennon explained to young people,] 'You've got the power. . . . All we have to do is remember that: we've all got the power. That's why we said, "War is over if you want it.". . . Don't believe that jazz that there's nothing you can do, "just turn on and drop out, man." You've got to turn on and drop *in*. Or they're going to drop all over you. . . . And if you're hip to that, you've got to make your parents hip to that. Instead of despising them, use some compassion.'"

John and Yoko bought billboard space in several cities as part of their "War Is Over" campaign.

was leaving the group. When the film *Let It Be* was released several weeks later, millions went to see the last glimmering moments of their favorite band.

PRIMAL SCREAM

Although Lennon had been contemplating leaving the Beatles for years, he was truly shattered when the band officially came to an end after McCartney's announcement. Lennon had yet to really contemplate life without the support of the other Beatles. Instead of feeling a sense of freedom, he felt a sense of loss. Taking to his mansion, the musician refused to speak to anybody and often spent the day in bed smoking marijuana and watching television. Even his relationship with Ono deteriorated.

One day a friend mailed Lennon a book called *The Primal Scream*, written by controversial psychiatrist Dr. Arthur Janov. In the book, Janov spells out a theory that states that all neurosis comes from a lack of parental love that some people feel when they are small children. To get people over these experiences and regain mental health, Janov helped his patients dredge up childhood memories until they began to scream and cry.

Lennon, who had been abandoned by both his mother and father, related to Janov's theory. Before long he was taking a five-month session in primal scream therapy from Janov in Los Angeles. All of Lennon's pain from the breakup of the band, from his childhood, and from the deaths of his mother, Stuart Sutcliffe, and Brian Epstein came pouring out of his soul.

Janov's therapy unleashed a hidden store of anger and pain in Lennon, which was reflected in his 1970 solo album, *Plastic Ono Band*. The tracks on the album ache with misery. In "Mother," Lennon asks where his mother and father have gone. In "Isolation" he explores his raw feelings of abandonment. In "God" Lennon, who had introduced the world to gurus and enlightenment, says he doesn't believe in yoga, the Beatles, Paul, Elvis, or Jesus, he just believes in Yoko. At the end, Lennon wistfully tells Beatles fans that the dream of Beatlemania is over.

In early 1971, as a followup to the album, Lennon was interviewed by Jann Wenner, editor of *Rolling Stone* magazine. In the long, scathing interview, he bared his soul, at first saying "I wish I was a fisherman . . . I'd sooner be poor than rich"[97] before lashing out at the Beatles, Beatlemania, and others.

SONGS FOR A CAUSE

The early 1970s were tense times. The Vietnam War had stretched out longer than World War II, and people were polarized over the issue. Peaceful protests had not stopped the war, and antiwar protests were turning increasingly violent as students, police, and National Guardsmen clashed in bloody confrontations.

John Lennon and Yoko Ono put themselves in the midst of this turmoil, becoming outspoken critics of the war in Vietnam and other issues. To get the message across, the former Beatle once again used his fame and talent to spread his views.

National Guardsmen order protesters out of downtown Berkeley during an antiwar demonstration. Peaceful protests against the Vietnam War had been ineffective, and soon demonstrations became violent.

In May 1971, the same week that more than fifty thousand antiwar protesters marched on Washington, D.C., Lennon's "Power to the People" was number eleven on the Billboard charts. Jon Wiener describes the song in *Come Together: John Lennon in His Own Time:*

> John sang it as a street song, a marching song, a fighting song. This was a new world for him. In his earlier political song ["Give Peace a Chance"], "we" had asked our leaders to give peace "a chance." Now Lennon asserted that decisions should be made, not by those in power but rather by the people as a whole.[98]

Several months later, Lennon released the album *Imagine*, whose title song became one of the musician's best-loved solo efforts. In "Imagine," Lennon asks the listener to imagine a world with no heaven, no hell, no possessions, and no religion—just people living together in peace. While admitting he's a dreamer, Lennon asked people to join him and Ono in uniting the world. The sentiment and melodic beauty of "Imagine" helped make the album Lennon's first number one since leaving the Beatles.

TELEVISION TALK SHOW HOSTS

In February 1972, John Lennon and Yoko Ono made their longest and most publicized appearance when they cohosted the *Mike Douglas Show* for an entire week. This show was the highest-rated afternoon talk show in the country at the time, and the Lennons picked many of the guests that appeared on the show. They included Black Panther Bobby Seale, Yippie Jerry Rubin, consumer advocate Ralph Nader, and even rock legend Chuck Berry.

Lennon and Ono spent the week entertaining America and talking about love, peace, women's liberation, racial discrimination, the Vietnam War, and the U.S. prison system. One afternoon, Ono instituted a love project in which everyone was told to dial a telephone number at random and say "I love you" to the person who answered. To demonstrate, she dialed a phone number and, according to Jon Wiener in *Come Together: John Lennon in His Own Time*, told a startled woman, "This is Yoko. I love you. Please pass this message along."

The most radical moment of television history up to that time occurred when Lennon introduced Jerry Rubin as a hero, and the Yippie leader told daytime audiences,

> We've got to get Nixon out of the White House. We've got to end the . . . warfare in Vietnam. . . . Everybody should register to vote—that's power, if we all vote together. We shouldn't vote for any candidate who doesn't withdraw everything from Vietnam. We ought to go to both [political] conventions, in Miami and San Diego, and nonviolently make our presence felt.

WORKING WITH THE YIPPIES

In August 1971, the Lennons decided to move to New York City, where they began to associate with antiwar leaders Abbie Hoffman and Jerry Rubin, the founders of the Yippies. Unlike other protest groups, the Yippies used humor and outrageous stunts to draw media attention to their cause. For instance, in 1968, the Yippies nominated a pig for president.

Lennon deeply appreciated this humorous approach to protest, and the feeling was mutual. As Rubin said, "[The] Yippies had been applying Beatles tactics to politics, trying to merge music and life. We talked about their bed-in as a Yippie action. . . . [We] were amazed at how we had been into the same kinds of things all these years."[99]

In late 1971, Lennon worked with Rubin and other Yippie leaders to put together a benefit concert for John Sinclair, a left-wing writer who had been jailed for ten years for possession of two marijuana cigarettes. Lennon believed the sentence was for Sinclair's support of antiwar causes, not for the small amount of drugs.

Lennon and Ono performed at the finale of the seven-hour concert, singing "John Sinclair," a song Lennon had written for the occasion about the plight of the man, whom he called a political prisoner. Incredibly, Sinclair was freed from prison two days after the concert when a judge overturned the long sentence. Although the legal maneuverings of Sinclair's lawyers actually gained his freedom, Lennon and Rubin were ecstatic.

Buoyed by this success, Rubin told the press that Lennon would perform at a huge concert, or a "political Woodstock," in San Diego, California, in August 1972 to protest the Republican Convention that was to be held there. Lennon, however, had never agreed to such a concert—he was afraid it would turn into a bloody riot. But it was too late. Rubin's announcement caught the attention of government authorities, who began an intense campaign against Lennon and Ono that would last for nearly four years.

GOVERNMENT INTERFERENCE

By early 1972, John Lennon was the target of a widespread—and illegal—campaign by the FBI, the CIA, and other government police organizations. His phones were tapped, he was followed by government agents, and his activities were recorded in thousands of pages of transcripts. FBI agents even wrote down words to songs Lennon sang in concert and classified them as top secret despite the fact that the lyrics were written on the album covers.

The U.S. government decided to use its full force to expel Lennon and Ono from the United States. In February 1972, Strom Thurmond, a Republican senator from South Carolina and a member of the Senate Internal Security Subcommittee, passed a memo to the U.S. attorney general John Mitchell that read,

> [Lennon, Rubin, and others] have devised a plan to hold rock concerts in various primary election states for the following purposes: to obtain access to college campuses; to press for legislation legalizing marijuana; to recruit persons to come to San Diego during the Republican National Convention in August 1972. . . .

> [Yippie leaders] intend to use John Lennon as a drawing card to promote their success. . . . This can only inevitably lead to a clash between a controlled mob organized by this group and law enforcement officials in San Diego. . . . If Lennon's visa is terminated it would be a strategic countermeasure.[100]

A few weeks later, the government revoked Lennon's visa and initiated deportation proceedings. Once again, the 1968 drug bust was used as an excuse.

While fighting deportation, Lennon and Ono became nervous wrecks. FBI agents were not subtle about following them. In fact, they wanted to frighten and intimidate the rock star and his wife.

Meanwhile, Lennon's lawyers solicited statements from dozens of respected musicians, actors, and artists, testifying to the musician's importance. Supporters included actors Fred Astaire and Tony Curtis, musician Stevie Wonder, artist Jasper Johns, and a slew of authors, including Norman Mailer, Saul Bellow, John Updike, and Kurt Vonnegut. Even Bob Dylan, who shunned publicity, contributed a note that said, "John and Yoko add a great voice and drive to this country's so called ART INSTITUTION. . . .

Hurray for John & Yoko. Let them stay and live here and breathe."[101]

"WHATEVER GETS YOU THROUGH THE NIGHT"

Despite the pleading of Lennon's fans, the government continued its action against the musician. As the case wound its way through various courts month after month, Lennon's political message was silenced by fear. Meanwhile, several multimillion-dollar lawsuits concerning the Beatles' pub-

The usually very private Bob Dylan submitted a note to Lennon's lawyer stating the important contributions John and Yoko made to American culture.

lishing rights and other Apple business continued to plague the singer.

The stress of the various trials and tribulations put an incredible strain on the Lennons' marriage. In September 1973 they separated, with John moving to Los Angeles and Yoko remaining in the couple's sprawling apartment in New York City's Dakota building.

In Los Angeles, Lennon's life disintegrated into a drunken debacle as he spent his days recording and his nights snorting cocaine and bar hopping. One night the singer was thrown out of the Troubadour nightclub for heckling the Smothers Brothers onstage. While being ejected from the club, Lennon tried to punch several people, including a photographer. The story got wide coverage in the press, and the promoter of peace and love began to look like a washed-up rock star.

While "acting out" in his pain and anger, however, Lennon was inspired to record two critically acclaimed albums—the 1973 *Mind Games* and the 1974 *Walls and Bridges*. Several songs on the albums hearkened back to Lennon's psychedelic '60s era, and although the words show a man in pain, the melody and production continue to prove Lennon's musical genius. One song, "Whatever Gets You Through the Night," became Lennon's first solo number-one single.

PEACE AND FAMILY

By 1974, President Richard Nixon had resigned from the presidency because of the Watergate burglary. John Mitchell, who had instigated the case against Lennon, was in jail for his role in Watergate. And the Viet-

Yoko stands between her son, Sean, and her stepson, Julian, in 1984.

nam War was nearly at an end. The Immigration and Naturalization Service, or INS, however, continued to pursue its case against the former Beatle.

In January 1975, Lennon and Ono resolved their marital conflicts, and Lennon moved back to New York City to reunite with his wife. He described the time he spent partying in L.A. as "the lost weekend that lasted eighteen months."[102] Soon after the couple were reunited, Ono became pregnant. Then, on October 7, the New York State Supreme Court reversed the deportation proceedings against Lennon, saying, "The court cannot condone selective deportation based upon secret political grounds."[103]

Two days later, on Lennon's thirty-fifth birthday, Yoko Ono gave birth to Sean Taro Ono Lennon, the couple's only child. In a role reversal highly uncommon in 1975,

Lennon decided to stay at home to raise his child, to become a "house-husband." Ono, in turn, took over the management of the musician's multimillion-dollar empire.

With permanent residence status and a new baby, John Lennon and Yoko Ono completely dropped out of the public eye. The world's biggest rock star spent his days changing diapers, baking bread, and cleaning up after the family cats.

"WE'RE ONE WORLD"

Between 1975 and 1979, by investing in real estate and even Holstein cows, Ono's business savvy had parlayed Lennon's formerly shaky finances into an empire worth hundreds of millions of dollars. One of Ono's investments was an oceanfront mansion in Palm Beach, Florida, where the couple celebrated their eleventh wedding anniversary on March 20, 1980. The vacation inspired Lennon to rent a sloop and sail to the Caribbean. On June 4, the inexperienced sailor left Rhode Island for Bermuda on a forty-three-foot sailboat manned by a seasoned crew. While fighting the wind, rain, and waves during a violent thunderstorm, Lennon had an epiphany—he would come out of retirement with a new album.

As he sailed through the Atlantic, songs began pouring forth from Lennon's pen. When he got to Bermuda, he called Ono on the phone to sing his new songs to her. Ono began writing songs of her own, and by August, the Lennons were at the Hit Factory in Manhattan recording *Double Fantasy*, their first album in six years.

According to those who were there, the recording sessions were incredible. Ono banished drugs and alcohol from the studio, and Lennon hadn't been that lucid since the early 1960s. There were no deadlines, no Beatles to argue with, no hysterical fans waiting outside, and no painful childhood memories to confront. A large photo of Sean was taped above the mixing board, and the music was simply Lennon and Ono in love. Plans were made for two more albums to be released during the coming years.

To publicize the album, which was to be released in November, the couple conducted a long, extensive interview with David Sheff of *Playboy* over the course of three weeks. They talked about everything from the meaning behind certain Beatles songs to their relationship, their son, and the new album. Although the psychedelic '60s seemed far away by 1980, Lennon had not changed his message, as he told *Playboy:*

> We're one world, one people whether we like it or not. Aren't we? I mean, we can pretend we're divided into races and countries and we can carry on pretending that until we stop doin' it. But the reality is that it is one world and it is one people.[104]

On October 9, Lennon celebrated his fortieth birthday and Sean his fifth. For their present, Ono paid a skywriter to leave a message of love over the streets of Manhattan. When *Double Fantasy* was released on November 17, bearing a picture of the Lennons kissing, millions of fans were ecstatic. As Coleman writes,

[When] he re-entered the recording studios, Lennon was at a mental peak. No other major rock star had achieved such intellectual and physical maturity yet maintained an aura of rugged warmth. . . . He confounded the cynics by returning with his own highly personal stance, that somehow reached out to old and new music fans. In defeating all the odds, John had also beaten the system that chewed artists up before spitting them out as tired and worn.[105]

The couple's 1980 record, Double Fantasy, *bears a picture of John and Yoko kissing. The album was well received, and two more were scheduled to be released in the coming years.*

John Lennon　　　Double Fantasy　　　Yoko Ono

THE BITTER END

By December 1980, John Lennon was riding high. His new album had been well received and was selling briskly. Still full of creative energy, he continued to work in the studio nearly every day from early afternoon until around eleven o'clock at night.

On December 8, Lennon and Ono were at the Hit Factory putting the final touches on Ono's soon-to-be-released single. It was a warm evening when the Lennons' limousine pulled up to the Dakota. Instead of dropping the couple off in the sheltered courtyard of the building, Lennon and Ono got out of the car on the street. A man's voice called out "Mr. Lennon?"[106] When Lennon turned his head, a crazed fan, Mark David Chapman, shot him in the back five times with a .38 revolver. Lennon's blood-spattered spectacles flew in the air and shattered on the ground as he fell. Within fifteen minutes, John Lennon was dead from a massive loss of blood. Yoko Ono later released a simple statement: "John loved and prayed for the human race. Please do the same for him."[107]

A fan leaves flowers at a memorial to John Lennon in Japan. Lennon's musical, political, and personal examples touched people throughout the world.

As news of Lennon's death spread, the world went into mourning. Ray Coleman, who had been Lennon's friend since the early 1960s, stated,

> As the news of his murder broke, the world's airwaves were filled with his music. Tragically, incredibly, the moment of his death was also the time he came alive in the minds of millions. He was guaranteed immortality on a scale that neither he, nor the world's ageing Beatles fans, would ever comprehend. Not since the murder of President John F. Kennedy in 1963 had the world been so enraged, stunned, and simply hurt by an assassination. Lennon's murder transcended that of even a major statesman because John was so much closer to his public. For one awful moment, a world that didn't care was brought together, and in its grief remembered *how* to care. As shock turned to anger, as statesmen paid their tributes to his talent and human qualities, as the Dakota flag hung at half mast in his honour, the bitter irony sank in: the rebel who had finally found tranquillity in his life and who had preached peace and love, offered hope, inspired millions with his imagination, self-deprecating wit, compassion, and new example of family commitment, had died by the gun.[108]

In the following days, millions gathered in public and private to mourn the passing of John Lennon. Lennon's boyhood home in Liverpool was surrounded by mourners. In London, Paris, and elsewhere, people gathered in parks with flowers, banners, pictures, and candles. More than 400,000 people came to honor Lennon in Central Park across from the Dakota as part of a worldwide ten-minute observation of silence. People remained outside the Dakota for days, as a makeshift memorial was established on the spot where Lennon had fallen. Ono went into mourning, refusing to leave her apartment. More than 250,000 letters of sympathy arrived at the Dakota, and more than 7 million copies of *Double Fantasy* sold within the next several months.

THE DREAM IS OVER

In the years since Lennon's death, his memory and music continue to be honored. In 1984, Ono dedicated Strawberry Fields, a small piece of land in Central Park, to honor John Lennon. And every year on December 8, fans gather there to remember the musician who meant so much to them.

Few words can describe the impact John Lennon had on the world with his music, his humor, and his profound dedication to love and peace. He was a man who was committed to making the world a better place, and he worked tirelessly to do so. He was always ahead of his time, steering his own course through the worlds of music, fashion, and politics. While others talked, Lennon acted, often at great personal expense to himself and his family.

John Lennon was abandoned by his father, suffered the death of his mother, had several of his best friends die, and was arrested, rejected, and ridiculed in the press. Through it all, though, his message remained unerringly positive. He remained true to himself and true to his vision until the very end. Today, John Lennon lives forever in music.

Notes

Introduction: A Message in Music

1. Quoted in Lorenza Muñoz, "From Lenin to Lennon: Cuba Honors Former Beatle," *Los Angeles Times*, December 12, 2000, p. F3.

Chapter 1: Life in Liverpool

2. Quoted in Philip Norman, *Shout.* New York: Simon and Schuster, 1981, p. 18.

3. Quoted in The Beatles, *The Beatles Anthology.* San Francisco: Chronicle Books, 2000, p. 7.

4. Quoted in Albert Goldman, *The Lives of John Lennon.* New York: William Morrow, 1988, p. 35.

5. Goldman, *The Lives of John Lennon*, pp. 36–37.

6. Quoted in The Beatles, *The Beatles Anthology*, p. 7.

7. Quoted in Ray Coleman, *Lennon.* New York: McGraw-Hill, 1984, p. 25.

8. Quoted in Coleman, *Lennon*, p. 23.

9. Norman, *Shout*, p. 21.

10. Quoted in Coleman, *Lennon*, p. 30.

11. Quoted in Norman, *Shout*, p. 23.

12. Pete Shotton and Nicholas Schaffner, *John Lennon in My Life.* New York: Stein and Day, 1983, p. 31.

13. Quoted in The Beatles, *The Beatles Anthology*, p. 20.

14. Quoted in The Beatles, *The Beatles Anthology*, pp. 8–9.

15. Norman, *Shout*, p. 24.

16. Shotton and Schaffner, *John Lennon in My Life*, p. 33.

17. John Lennon, *Lennon Remembers.* San Francisco: Straight Arrow Books, 1971, pp. 64–65.

18. Quoted in The Beatles, *The Beatles Anthology*, p. 8.

19. Quoted in Coleman, *Lennon*, p. 50.

20. Quoted in The Beatles, *The Beatles Anthology*, p. 10.

21. Norman, *Shout*, p. 25.

22. Norman, *Shout*, p. 33.

23. Shotton and Schaffner, *John Lennon in My Life*, p. 49.

24. Quoted in Norman, *Shout*, p. 35.

25. Quoted in The Beatles, *The Beatles Anthology*, p. 11.

26. Quoted in The Beatles, *The Beatles Anthology*, p. 8.

Chapter 2: Learning to Rock and Roll

27. Quoted in Norman, *Shout*, p. 35.

28. Shotton and Schaffner, *John Lennon in My Life*, p. 48.

29. Shotton and Schaffner, *John Lennon in My Life*, p. 51.

30. Norman, *Shout*, p. 36.

31. Quoted in Shotton and Schaffner, *John Lennon in My Life*, p. 53.

32. Quoted in Coleman, *Lennon*, p. 65.

33. Shotton and Schaffner, *John Lennon in My Life*, p. 53.

34. Quoted in The Beatles, *The Beatles Anthology*, p. 20.

35. Quoted in Shotton and Schaffner, *John Lennon in My Life*, p. 56.

36. Quoted in Norman, *Shout*, pp. 44–45.

37. Quoted in The Beatles, *The Beatles Anthology*, p. 20.

38. Quoted in The Beatles, *The Beatles Anthology*, p. 20.

39. Coleman, *Lennon*, p. 89.

40. Quoted in The Beatles, *The Beatles Anthology*, p. 13.

Chapter 3: Becoming a Star

41. Shotton and Schaffner, *John Lennon in My Life*, p. 65.

42. Quoted in Coleman, *Lennon*, p. 124.

43. Shotton and Schaffner, *John Lennon in My Life*, p. 68.

44. Brian Epstein, *A Cellar Full of Noise*. New York: Byron Press Multimedia, 1998, p. 97.

45. Quoted in Shotton and Schaffner, *John Lennon in My Life*, p. 69.

46. Epstein, *A Cellar Full of Noise*, p. 98.

47. Quoted in The Beatles, *The Beatles Anthology*, p. 65.

48. Quoted in The Beatles, *The Beatles Anthology*, p. 67.

49. Quoted in Coleman, *Lennon*, p. 158.

50. Quoted in Coleman, *Lennon*, p. 162.

51. Quoted in The Beatles, *The Beatles Anthology*, p. 67.

52. Quoted in The Beatles, *The Beatles Anthology*, p. 67.

53. Quoted in The Beatles, *The Beatles Anthology*, p. 70.

54. Quoted in The Beatles, *The Beatles Anthology*, p. 72.

55. Shotton and Schaffner, *John Lennon in My Life*, p. 72.

56. Quoted in The Beatles, *The Beatles Anthology*, p. 73.

57. Quoted in Coleman, *Lennon*, p. 194.

58. Quoted in Shotton and Schaffner, *John Lennon in My Life*, p. 80.

59. Coleman, *Lennon*, p. 196.

Chapter 4: Beatlemania

60. Shotton and Schaffner, *John Lennon in My Life*, p. 89.

61. Quoted in Fred Bronson, *The Billboard Book of Number One Hits*. New York: Billboard Publications, 1988, p. 143.

62. Bronson, *The Billboard Book of Number One Hits*, p. 143.

63. Quoted in The Beatles, *The Beatles Anthology*, p. 116.

64. Quoted in The Beatles, *The Beatles Anthology*, p. 119.

65. Quoted in Coleman, *Lennon*, p. 214.

66. Quoted in Coleman, *Lennon*, p. 214.

67. Norman, *Shout*, p. 240.

68. Quoted in Coleman, *Lennon*, p. 244.

69. Coleman, *Lennon*, p. 245.

70. Quoted in The Beatles, *The Beatles Anthology*, p. 158.

71. Quoted in The Beatles, *The Beatles Anthology*, p. 177.

72. Quoted in Coleman, *Lennon*, p. 322.

73. Quoted in The Beatles, *The Beatles Anthology*, p. 223.

74. Quoted in The Beatles, *The Beatles Anthology*, p. 227.

75. Quoted in The Beatles, *The Beatles Anthology*, p. 229.

Chapter 5: Idealism, Energy, Music, and Money

76. Mark Lewisohn, *The Beatles Recording Sessions*. New York: Harmony Books, 1988, p. 70.

77. George Martin, *With a Little Help from My Friends: The Making of Sgt. Pepper*. New York: Little, Brown, 1994, p. 24.

78. Martin, *With a Little Help from My Friends*, p. 157.

79. Norman, *Shout*, p. 294.

80. Quoted in Norman, *Shout*, pp. 292–93.

81. Quoted in Norman, *Shout*, p. 293.

82. Quoted in The Beatles, *The Beatles Anthology*, p. 260.

83. Quoted in The Beatles, *The Beatles Anthology*, p. 262.

84. Quoted in The Beatles, *The Beatles Anthology*, p. 267.

85. Quoted in Shotton and Schaffner, *John Lennon in My Life*, p. 156.

86. Lennon, *Lennon Remembers*, p. 56.

87. Shotton and Schaffner, *John Lennon in My Life*, p. 158.

88. Quoted in G. Barry Golson, ed., *The Playboy Interviews with John Lennon and Yoko Ono*. New York: Playboy Press, 1981, p. 158.

89. Jerry Hopkins, *Yoko Ono*. New York: Macmillan, 1986, p. 79.

90. Quoted in Golson, *The Playboy Interviews with John Lennon and Yoko Ono*, p. 122.

91. Quoted in Hopkins, *Yoko Ono*, p. 79.

92. Lennon, *Lennon Remembers*, p. 51.

93. Quoted in Shotton and Schaffner, *John Lennon in My Life*, p. 176.

94. Quoted in Hopkins, *Yoko Ono*, p. 82.

Chapter 6: John and Yoko

95. Quoted in The Beatles, *The Beatles Anthology*, p. 333.

96. Quoted in The Beatles, *The Beatles Anthology*, p. 333.

97. Lennon, *Lennon Remembers*, p. 11.

98. Jon Wiener, *Come Together: John Lennon in His Own Time*. New York: Random House, 1984, p. 155.

99. Quoted in Wiener, *Come Together*, p. 174.

100. Quoted in Wiener, *Come Together*, p. 225.

101. Quoted in Wiener, *Come Together*, pp. 237–38.

102. Quoted in Golson, *The Playboy Interviews with John Lennon and Yoko Ono*, p. 20.

103. Quoted in Coleman, *Lennon*, p. 621.

104. Quoted in Golson, *The Playboy Interviews with John Lennon and Yoko Ono*, p. 16.

105. Coleman, *Lennon*, p. 578.

106. Quoted in Coleman, *Lennon*, p. 583.

107. Quoted in Coleman, *Lennon*, p. 584.

108. Coleman, *Lennon*, p. 584.

For Further Reading

The Beatles, *The Beatles Anthology*. San Francisco: Chronicle Books, 2000. Four hundred large pages of rare photos and insightful text by the Beatles about the Beatles. As the book's dust cover says, "The Beatles' story told for the first time in their own words and pictures."

G. Barry Golson, ed., *The Playboy Interviews with John Lennon and Yoko Ono*. New York: Playboy Press, 1981. An extensive interview with Lennon and Ono in which Lennon discusses all aspects of his life and work. The former Beatle was assassinated only days after the interviews were completed.

Stuart Kallen, *Renaissance of Rock: The British Invasion*. Minneapolis: Abdo & Daughters, 1989. The story of the Beatles and other popular English rock bands that became superstars during the British musical invasion of the 1960s.

Michael Kronenwetter, *America in the 1960s*. San Diego: Lucent Books, 1998. Discusses a decade of enormous change and conflict in all areas of life, including science, civil rights, social welfare, national defense, politics, and the arts.

John Lennon, *In His Own Write and A Spaniard in the Works*. New York: New American Library, 1967. Lennon's zany short stories and cartoonlike drawings originally released in 1964 and 1965 as two separate best-selling books.

———, *Lennon Remembers*. San Francisco: Straight Arrow Books, 1971. A long and revealing interview with *Rolling Stone* magazine publisher Jann Wenner conducted shortly after the breakup of the Beatles. Lennon discusses the Beatles' success, the meaning behind some of his lyrics, the pain he suffered during his childhood, his relationship with Yoko Ono, and the breakup of the Beatles.

Marvin Martin, *The Beatles: The Music Was Never the Same*. New York: Franklin Watts, 1996. A biography of the four "Lads from Liverpool" who achieved phenomenal success as the Beatles and endured the intense pressure of international fame.

Tom Stockdale, *John Lennon*. Philadelphia: Chelsea House, 1998. Presents the life of John Lennon, from his early years through the rise and breakup of the Beatles to his final days in New York.

Mike Venezia, *The Beatles*. New York: Childrens Press, 1997. The story of the world's most celebrated and influential rock group.

Adam Woog, *The Beatles*. San Diego: Lucent Books, 1998. A book that details the cultural significance, influence, and legacy of the Beatles from the "Importance Of" series.

Works Consulted

Books and Periodicals

"Beatles Top RIAA List," *Rolling Stone*, Issue 864, March 15, 2001. A short article revealing that the Beatles are the top-selling recording artists of all time.

Fred Bronson, *The Billboard Book of Number One Hits*. New York: Billboard Publications, 1988. *Billboard* is a trade magazine dedicated to the music and entertainment business. It introduced the first "music popularity chart" in 1940, and by the 1950s the magazine featured a weekly list of the Top 100 selling songs. With twenty listings, the Beatles have the most number-one hits in the book.

Lewis Carroll, *The Complete Works of Lewis Carroll*. New York: Modern Library, 1985. A book containing the classic children's story *Alice's Adventures in Wonderland* and dozens of other short stories by Lewis Carroll. Lennon often claimed that he was inspired by Carroll and modeled some of his song lyrics after the words of this famous children's author.

Ray Coleman, *Lennon*. New York: McGraw-Hill, 1984. A definitive biography of John Lennon written by an editor of *Melody Maker*, a popular British music magazine. The author first became friends with Lennon in 1962 and wrote this biography with the cooperation of the ex-Beatles' family and friends.

Brian Epstein, *A Cellar Full of Noise*. New York: Byron Press Multimedia, 1998. The autobiography of Brian Epstein details his early life and his success with the Beatles and other top '60s groups; it was originally released in 1967 shortly before his untimely death.

Albert Goldman, *The Lives of John Lennon*. New York: William Morrow, 1988. One of the most negative books ever written about Lennon; it attempts to explore his "dark side" by using pop psychology and negative gossip perpetrated by his enemies.

Jerry Hopkins, *Yoko Ono*. New York: Macmillan, 1986. An unauthorized biography of John Lennon's second wife by a journalist who has written the life stories of Elvis Presley, the Doors, Jimi Hendrix, David Bowie, and others.

Mark Lewisohn, *The Beatles Recording Sessions*. New York: Harmony Books, 1988. A definitive book of the Beatles recording sessions with dates, technical details, and a revealing insider look at how the band achieved their unsurpassed sounds in the studio.

George Martin, *With a Little Help from My Friends: The Making of Sgt. Pepper*. New York: Little, Brown, 1994. This book details the technical and creative processes behind the Beatles' most highly acclaimed masterpiece, written by the producer who was instrumental in shaping those sounds.

Lorenza Muñoz, "From Lenin to Lennon: Cuba Honors Former Beatle," *Los Angeles Times*, December 12, 2000. An article about the memorial park in Cuba dedicated to Lennon on the twentieth anniversary of his death.

Philip Norman, *Shout*. New York: Simon and Schuster, 1981. The definitive biography on the Beatles, from their childhood lives in Liverpool through their years as chart-topping rock royalty, written by a journalist from the *London Times* who traveled with the group extensively in the late 1960s.

Pete Shotton and Nicholas Schaffner, *John Lennon in My Life*. New York: Stein and Day, 1983. An insider's perspective of the former Beatle by a man who first met John Lennon at the age of five. Shotton and Lennon remained extremely close friends until the musician's death in 1980.

Jon Wiener, *Come Together: John Lennon in His Own Time*. New York: Random House, 1984. Wiener, a history professor, spent years researching the intimidation and harassment the FBI and CIA directed against John Lennon for his political views. This book is taken from twenty-six pounds of federal documents and dossiers on Lennon and details the extent to which Lennon was a target of illegal U.S. government actions in the 1970s.

Websites

Artist Direct, "George Harrison Biography," 2001, http://ubl.artistdirect.com/fp2.asp?layout=a_bio&artistid=00225. A website dedicated to George Harrison from Artist Direct with links relating to Harrison news, musical downloads, CD reviews, products, and other related information.

The Beatles.com, 2000, www.beatles.com/top.html. The Beatles' own website, promoting their 2000 album *1*, features information about all their number-one songs, live clips of the band, studio archives, album sleeves, international press releases, a virtual gallery, a trivia quiz, and a Yellow Submarine video game.

Frank Daniels, "The Beatles with Tony Sheridan," Across the Universe, 2000, www.scs.unr.edu/~fdaniels/stuff/tony.htm. A Web page by a dedicated Beatle fan with articles, record jackets, photos, and other paraphernalia concerning the Fab Four.

National Trust, "The Early Years," 2000, www.spekehall.org.uk/early_years.htm. A virtual tour of Paul McCartney's childhood home, with information about his youth; the website is run by Great Britain's National Trust, a guardian for the nation in the acquisition and protection of threatened coastline, countryside, and buildings.

Rocking Pete, "The Velvet Collar and the Iron Fist," The Teddy Boy Movement, n.d., www.rockabilly.nl/general/teddyboys.htm. A website dedicated to the styles, music, and history of the English Teddy Boy movement of the 1950s and '60s, along with its rockabilly resurgence in the '80s and '90s.

Gary Shultz, "Ringo Starr Biography—Early Years," Ringo Home Page, November 20, 2000, http://web2.airmail.net/gshultz/bio1.html. A website dedicated to Ringo Starr, featuring his biography, drumming tips, discography, solo career, and other items.

Index

Picture Credits

Cover photo: © Bob Whitaker/Camera Press/Retna Limited, USA

© AFP/Corbis, 10, 98

Archive Photos, 20 (both), 53

Bettmann Archive, 76

© Bettmann/Corbis, 19, 33, 35, 54 (right), 57, 67, 81, 87, 89, 94, 95, 97

Michael Browne, 36, 40

CBS Photo/Archive/Archive Photos, 51

Express Newspapers/Archive Photos, 54 (left)

Express Newspapers/L-166/Archive Photos, 79

FPG International, 8, 9

© Farrell Grehan/Corbis, 14, 48

© Hulton-Deutsch Collection/Corbis, 13, 23, 26, 31, 45, 47

© Douglas Kirkland/Corbis, 73

Photofest, 42, 58, 62, 74, 83

Popperfoto/Archive Photos, 56, 63, 65

William L. Rukeyser/Archive Photos, 91

© Ted Streshinsky/Corbis, 75

Catherine Ursillo/Archive Photos, 71

About the Author

Stuart A. Kallen is the author of more than 150 nonfiction books for children and young adults. He has written on topics ranging from the theory of relativity to rock 'n' roll history to life on the American frontier. In addition, Mr. Kallen has written award-winning children's videos and television scripts. In his spare time, Stuart A. Kallen is a singer/songwriter/guitarist in San Diego, California.